THE ART OF
BIEDERMEIER

THE ART OF
BIEDERMEIER

DOMINIC R. STONE

CHARTWELL
BOOKS, INC.

A QUINTET BOOK

Published by Chartwell Books
A Division of Book Sales, Inc.
110 Enterprise Avenue
Secaucus, New Jersey 07094

ISBN 1–55521–570–X

This book was designed and produced by
Quintet Publishing Limited
6 Blundell Street
London N7 9BH

Creative Director: Peter Bridgewater
Art Director: Ian Hunt
Designer: James Lawrence
Project Editor: Caroline Beattie
Editor: Barbara Fuiler
Picture Researcher: Shona Wood

Typeset in Great Britain by
Central Southern Typesetters, Eastbourne
Manufactured in Hong Kong by
Regent Publishing Services Limited
Printed in Hong Kong by
Leefung-Asco Printers Limited

CONTENTS

1.   Introduction: The Biedermeier Age . . . 7

2.   Biedermeier Life: Viennese Culture and Society 1815–1845 . . . 15

3.   Furniture in the Biedermeier Period . . . 31

4.   Biedermeier Ceramics and Glass . . . 61

5.   Biedermeier Architecture, Interiors and Domestic Life . . . 79

6.   Decorative and Applied Arts in the Biedermeier Era . . . 97

7.   Biedermeier Art: Painting in Oils and Watercolours . . . 111

8.   Conclusion: The Biedermeier Legacy . . . 123

Index . . . 126

INTRODUCTION: THE BIEDERMEIER AGE

Many people who have even a passing interest in antique furniture will have heard of the Biedermeier style. It is a term often used – and occasionally misused – when describing a particular type of furniture from the German-speaking nations in the early nineteenth century. It brings to mind an image of simplicity which is at the same time sumptuous; a kind of calm self-assurance in decoration which can sometimes have a startlingly modern appearance. Bold, adventurous designs which eschew the intricacy and fussiness of earlier styles, and quotes from the language of Classical architecture which at times seem to have an almost theatrical quality, characterize furniture in the Biedermeier style. But what is Biedermeier? Where did it come from, and how can one recognize its features? Is it in fact a style, or a period in history?

In fact, the definition of Biedermeier, and its chronological, stylistic and geographical limits has been the source of an arcane, long-running debate which has been conducted by mostly German and Austrian art historians for several decades. What concerns us here is not this quarrel, but rather the superlative decorative arts which emerged from a unique period in European history. The playful and inventive designs for furniture which emanated from the Danhauser Furniture Factory in Vienna, the skill of the Bohemian glass-blowers and engravers, the superbly proportioned architecture of Karl Friedrich Schinkel in Berlin; all these and more besides are manifestations of the Biedermeier culture. As one delves deeper into this field – one which is relatively unexplored, in the English language – it becomes clear that it covers more than just a surface appearance. These crafts are the result of an idea, a way of life; the same attitude which produced the music of Beethoven and Schubert, and the literature of Adalbert Stifter.

THE NAME 'BIEDERMEIER'

'Biedermeier' as a choice of term for describing the art and culture of the German-speaking states in the first half of the nineteenth century is laden with irony, of both the conscious and unconscious varieties. The word 'Biedermeier' is taken from the pseudonym of the writers Adolph Kussmaul (1822–1902) and Ludwig Eichrodt (1827–1892), who wrote for a

ABOVE: *James Baker Payne (1800–70): View of Heidelberg, with the castle in the foreground. Watercolour.*

LEFT: *William Wyld (1806–89): Dresden.*

satirical magazine, *Fliegende Blätter* (Flying Leaves); it is in fact spelt 'Biedermaier' in this form. It was coined as a name for an imaginary author, Gottlob Biedermaier, whose work was intended to symbolize the attitudes and aspirations of his generation. '*Bieder*' is a German word meaning common or garden, everyday, plain; 'Meier' (or Maier) is a common German surname, equivalent to Smith.

As with so many names coined as scornful or derogatory descriptions of artistic and cultural movements of the past – Baroque, Rococo, and Gothic, for example – the term, in its original meaning, was far from complementary. It was intended as a heavily sarcastic label, whose use was at first confined to literature, and later was extended to cover fine and applied arts, for all that was regarded as having been backwards and insular in the short period in Austria's history known as the *Vormärz*, or Pre-March, era. This covered the years between 1815, when the Congress of Vienna was held, and 1848, when the events in France sixty years previously finally caught up with the Austrian Empire and triggered a revolution.

THE BIEDERMEIER PERIOD

The Congress of Vienna, a meeting of the five major powers of Europe which took place between 1814 and 1815, brought an end to the Napoleonic Wars which had ravaged the continent since 1799. It ushered in a new period of peace and security in central Europe, and the Austrian Empire gained considerably from this settlement. Long-standing territorial disputes were settled, and at the cost of some compromise in this sphere, the Danube Monarchy was able to preside over a more prosperous and calm empire, and to dominate most of the small confederate states which are now modern-day West and East Germany. The Napoleonic Wars had been financially ruinous for Austria, so much so that a law had been passed requiring all citizens to surrender their silver and gold for melting down, in order to help pay for the war effort. The sporadic and unpredictable nature of combat had created a lack of confidence in the state and had lowered morale among traders and merchants.

The new age of peace brought security and prosperity: it also demanded sacrifices, however. The authorities of the Austrian Empire – a huge swathe of land, occupying all of present-day Austria, Hungary, and most of what is now western Czechoslovakia (Bohemia) – were apprehensive of the possibility of the spread of the French Revolution of 1789 to their own empire, and therefore kept a tight rein on political activities and publishing. The censor's power was almost unbounded; books, pamphlets, illustrations and plays all had to be submitted for scrutiny, and there were restrictions on travel and the import of printed material into the cities. At the same time, a new, much larger bourgeoisie arose with the opening up of trade between Austria and her erstwhile enemies, including France, Prussia, and Britain. The members of this class of merchants and well-to-do professional people became the typical Biedermeier citizens: relatively wealthy, predominantly urban, and preoccupied with domestic comfort and security. They were denied any great opportunity for political expression, although it is fair to say that this hardly seemed to matter; most of them, enjoying an unprecedented era of economic growth and rising living standards, and mindful of the horrors of the recent past, had little appetite for confrontation and conflict. Instead, they poured their efforts into the home and the family, into domestic crafts and art, and into music and society gatherings. The

RIGHT TOP: A Ranftbecher, *or decorative glass, with a portrait of the Duke of Reichstadt, by Anton Kothgasser, c1832.*

RIGHT BELOW: A Ranftbecher, *gilded and with a depiction of the St Stephan's cathedral in Vienna. This view was an extremely popular choice of subject matter for these decorative pieces.*

ABOVE: Samuel Prout (1783–1852):
Cologne, with the famous
cathedral in the background.

impulse of a new class of patrons revived and invigorated the traditionally rich crafts of the region, and were the central influence on the birth of a new style, which was distinct from the extravagance and ostentation of the earlier Baroque and Rococo fashions. As wealth became more widely spread, the tendency for 'conspicuous consumption', the desire for display, receded and was instead replaced by an emphasis on comfort and practicality.

Biedermeier furniture and interior decoration has enjoyed an upsurge in popularity in Britain and the United States in recent years. In continental Europe, by contrast, it has exerted a virtually continuous influence on architects and designers since its 're-discovery' at the beginning of this century. The style has been championed by legendary figures such as Josef Hoffmann and the Swiss architect Le Corbusier. There is still an uncertainty however about precisely what constitutes the Biedermeier style, and which objects can reasonably described as being representative of it. The vagueness which surrounds the whole area is understandable when one considers the historical and geographical origins of the term. To further confuse matters, there have been several 'revivals' of the style; in fact, interest in Biedermeier has grown steadily since almost immediately after the style 'ended' in 1848, so one can hardly speak of a revival as such. Knowledge of the artists and craftsmen working in the Biedermeier era has been amassed gradually, so that what we have now is a remarkable picture of an equally remarkable period in the history of what was once the cultural and political centre of Europe.

TWO

BIEDERMEIER LIFE: VIENNESE CULTURE AND SOCIETY 1815–1848

The political aspect of life between the Congress of Vienna of 1814–15, and the Revolution of 1848, is often described as the *Vormärz*, or Pre-March, era; a time of strict political and social restriction. The art and culture of the time – those aspects of the Pre-March period we refer to as Biedermeier life – undoubtedly owe many of their particular traits to these political undercurrents. There are also interesting contrasts however between these two aspects of contemporary life, since in many ways they were contradictory. While political activity remained dormant, restrained by the heavy hand of the police, cultural activity of all kinds flourished. Life in the period following the Congress of Vienna bore the indelible stamp of the censor (in the case of prints and texts, often literally), as the authorities attempted to resist the winds of change that had been blowing through the European Continent since the French Revolution in 1789. To understand the almost pathological fear of revolution and insurrection displayed by Prince Metternich – the key figure in the Austrian administration for more than three decades – and his allies, and the consequences this was to have for contemporary Austrian life, it is necessary to look briefly at the history of the region around the time of the Congress of 1814–15.

THE HISTORICAL BACKGROUND

In the closing years of the eighteenth century, Prussia and Russia both made gradual gains of territory, mostly at the expense of Poland. The Austrian Empire, covering modern-day Austria, Hungary, and western Czechoslovakia, was forced to come to terms with its vast (and increasingly powerful) imperial neighbour, the Russian Empire. Austria and Prussia endeavoured to form independent alliances with Russia; the long-standing political and territorial rivalry between the two countries meant that each would have much to gain from this partnership. The sporadic wars and skirmishes in the region were contributing to the financial hardship of the Austrian Empire, and isolating it from foreign trade and culture. Against this backdrop of tension, the French Revolution brought a new and different threat to the ruling powers in Vienna. The fear of attack from within, a popular uprising against the Monarchy and the Aristocracy, was taken very seriously indeed by Prince Clemens Lothar Metternich (1773–1859), the Austrian diplomat and Foreign Minister who played the central role in establishing the Congress of Vienna. Paris had been overrun by the Allies – including Russia, Prussia, and Austria – on 31 March, 1814, and Napoleon had abdicated shortly afterwards, creating a new vacuum of political leadership and military superiority in Europe.

RIGHT: A commode in fruitwood and walnut. The applied carving of this piece is particularly elaborate; note also the playful decoration to the feet.

LEFT: A table in birchwood, Sweden, c1830–40.

The Congress was in effect a peace conference, which was attended by representatives of almost all of the European States, and was intended from Austria's point of view to establish 'legitimacy', or the God-given right of the Emperor to govern, and to unite the five major nations in a balance of power which would oppose revolutionary tendencies. One of the ironies of this situation was that the Emperor himself, Francis I (1768–1835), felt powerless to influence the deeds that were to be carried out in his name, such was Metternich's hold over the Austrian administration. The concept of legitimacy has been attributed variously to Prince Charles Maurice de Talleyrand (1754–1838), a member of Napoleon's government in Paris, and to Metternich himself; there is little doubt however that both men were equally convinced of the necessity of monarchy to maintain peace and order. The five main states attending the Congress – Austria, Russia, Britain, Prussia and France – agreed on a series of compromises which brought an end to the hostilities of the Napoleonic Wars and generally stabilized foreign relations between European nations for the first time in decades, enabling greater social and cultural development to take place. One of the most important principles of the Congress was to restore the political situation which pertained in 1792, that is to say, before Napoleon's territorial gains.

RIGHT: Carl Spitzweg (1808–85):
Der Sonntagsjager *(The Sunday*
Hunter), 1844, oils on canvas.
This humorous painting could
almost depict the original
Herr Beidermeier; *a solid,*
unpretentious, affluent burgher,
with a hankering after the rural
life, but totally out of his depth,
playing Lord of the Manor in
a forest.

To Metternich, however, this new stability abroad merely heightened the alternative danger of growing internal political unrest and opposition, and so, in September 1815, the Holy Alliance was established. This was a union of national governments – among them Catholic Austria, Greek Orthodox Russia, and Protestant Prussia – who based their claim to govern on a divine right from God; again, the result for Austria was a kind of stifled internal stability, at the cost of civil liberties and free speech. A further outcome of the Congress was the establishment of the Germanic Confederation, a political union of 39 states, including Austria, which dominated the proceedings, and Prussia. The final outcome of the Congress was to establish Austria, and Vienna in particular, as the political and cultural centre of the region, a role which was to profoundly affect the development of Biedermeier culture in the following three decades.

THE POLITICAL CLIMATE

This 'government by divine right' was implemented in Austria by means of an authoritarian system of control and censorship of all publications and performances which could in any way be deemed political. This to the Austrian people must have seemed a small price to pay for release from the austerity and fear of the war years. The idea of censorship was by no means new: it had existed in Austria for some time, but was intensified in the period immediately after the Congress. The official censors, the Royal Imperial Central Book Checking Office, had a remarkably wide brief: not only printed media with an obviously political potential, such as books, pamphlets, and journals, but also prints and theatrical pieces, were all subjected to close examination. In addition, the draconian regulations covered other works with little or no immediately apparent subversive potential, such as maps, street signs, and other publicly displayed texts. Even well-established and highly regarded writers and illustrators were subject to restrictions which often appeared arbitrary and calculated to generate an atmosphere of intimidation and encourage self-censorship.

The activities of the Austrian secret police extended well beyond monitoring publications and printed matter. Particularly in the cities, informants were everywhere; it was seen as one's patriotic duty to listen in on private conversations, and, if necessary, to report their content to

the authorities. A mild sense of persecution was not unjustified in a system which felt itself threatened by even the most minor criticism; hence most discussions of a political nature were likely to be held in the safety of one's own home. In any case, relieved by the lifting of the threat of war, and enjoying the fruits of a cultural and commercial regeneration, the burgeoning middle classes – initially, at least – had little appetite for political organization and activity.

A recurring theme in the official justification for what certainly seemed to some artists and writers unnecessarily strict and oppressive control over their work was the insistence on the importance of peace and social harmony. The intention was therefore not purely cynical: Metternich, and his colleague Friedrich von Gentz, genuinely believed that the only way to avoid the carnage and destruction which had followed the events in France two and a half decades previously was to mould political aspirations into support for a well-defined, traditional monarchical state. Furthermore, the authorities' efforts to create a passive attitude among the bourgeoisie seem to have been met with success for the larger part of the Biedermeier age; attention turned away from the public sphere, and focussed instead on the family, the home and domestic life in general. Hobbies and pastimes assumed a new importance, as did domestic crafts such as needlework and embroidery. The caricature of the typical bourgeois citizen in the Pre-March period would have him exhibit all those characteristics upon which so much scorn would later be heaped. Herr Biedermeier was painted as being a modest man, unpretentious but rather dull, knowing what he liked and liking what he knew. He was eminently respectable, if rather unimaginative; in short, a solid, dependable member of the community, who was too concerned with his own little world to pay any heed to dangerous talk of revolution and international affairs.

RIGHT: A sofa table in birchwood, and two chairs, with ebonized inlay, Sweden, c1830. The gilt mounts on the chair backs reflect the lingering influence of the Empire style. The oil painting, of a birch forest, is Russian, and dates from the same era.

CULTURAL LIFE

In contrast to the picture of complacency and insularity given by the political side of Biedermeier life, the cultural and aesthetic aspects were charged with a new dynamism and vigour. Vienna became a cosmopolitan centre of commerce, education and society life. Many craftsmen from the provinces and from the German states converged on the city to

RIGHT: *Emil Jacob Schindler: Sunlight through Pine Trees, watercolour and gouache.*

LEFT: *Anonymous: landscape, oils, early 19th century. This picture is indicative in many ways of the Biedermeier feeling for the countryside. It combines a grand scale and sense of depth, with an idealized view of those living in the countryside.*

complete their apprenticeships and to set up workshops there. Working practices in the crafts, among them textiles, cabinet-making, and ceramics and glass, were in a state of flux for much of the first half of the eighteenth century, as the the power of the old established guilds and trade associations began to lessen and was replaced by the fundamentally different imperatives of factory production. Although not a large city by modern standards – less than 300,000 people lived in the city as a whole – Vienna was able to sustain a lively interchange of new fashions from abroad. It boasted several private and state-run schools and colleges, among them the *Wiener Polytechnische Institut* (a technical college), the *Akademie der Bildenen Künste* (The Academy of Fine Arts), and Karl Schmidt's esteemed drawing school. The lifting of trade bans and easing of transport difficulties which had hampered commercial development in the fifteen years preceding the Congress gave fresh impetus to artists and craftsmen across the Austrian Empire; competition from English glassware in particular, and to a lesser extent English furniture, stimulated these trades and encouraged technical innovation.

The single aspect of Austrian culture which tends to be best remembered from this period is the work of its composers. Ludwig van Beethoven (1770–1827) and Franz Schubert (1797–1828) spring to mind; there were however a number of lesser talents – predominantly in Vienna – active at the time. The emphasis was largely on 'light' and dance music, rather than the more 'serious' work typical of Beethoven. Life as a professional composer was far from easy, since the patronage of the court on which composers had traditionally relied was withdrawn after the Congress of 1815. Publishing scores was an alternative to commissions as a way of making a living from music since the preoccupation with family life and the home encouraged many amateur pianists to attempt the less demanding pieces for themselves. Music was equally likely to be encountered at society gatherings, where the waltzes of Johann Strauß the Elder (1804–1849) laid the foundations for a picture of Viennese society life which endures to this day.

A fondness for the Austrian countryside, and the natural world generally, emerged in particular from the urban middle class. Population density was increasing in even well-to-do areas of Vienna. This can be seen as the motivation for the creation of parks and gardens in cities, such as Vienna's Prater and Berlin's Lustgarten. The discovery of the beauty of nature is strongly associated with the Romantic Movement of the late eighteenth and early nineteenth century, and particularly with the *Sturm und Drang* (Storm and Stress) poets and novelists in Germany and Austria, who were reacting against the Rationalist and scientific currents of the eighteenth century. The natural world even found greater representation in the home itself; there was a vogue for jardinières and naturalistic arrangements of indoor plants. The trend is even more visible in the paintings of the era; a popular subject was the mountainous rural landscape of the region. It seems that the steadily increasing urbanization and industrialization of the early nineteenth century had created a new sentimentality and nostalgia for the countryside. In the harsh, feudal and agrarian life that had been led by the majority of the population in the preceding century, such a rosy, romantic view of a rural idyll would scarcely have been tenable.

The artists who suffered most under the censorship laws of Pre-March Austria were without doubt the writers. Many of the novelists and poets of the period responded to the restrictions placed on their work in a similar fashion to that of the rest of society: they concerned themselves with the home and the family, with art, and with detail. The most famous writer of the period, Adalbert Stifter (1805–1868), actually enjoyed his most productive period at the end of the Biedermeier era. His prose in particular illustrates the Biedermeier penchant for nature and the natural world, a tendency which had been absorbed from the chronologically and geographically much broader movement of Romanticism. His essay *Wien und die Wiener, in Bildern aus dem Leben* (Vienna and the Viennese, in Pictures from Life), is a revealing account of the city and its inhabitants in the years before the Revolution of 1848. Another writer, Franz Grillparzer (1791–1872), is chiefly remembered for his plays; his work *König Ottokars Glück und Ende* (King Ottokar's Fortune and Decline) was prevented from being performed for two years by the official censor, due to its allegedly political nature.

FACTORS OF CHANGE

An important factor which had an increasing effect on society throughout the Biedermeier era was the gradual industrialization and mechanization of industry. The industrial revolution took a much slower hold in Austria and the German states than in Britain; in 1816, more than ninety per cent of the region's population was rural. Imports of machinery and ideas from England and France did bring about significant changes in such fields as the production of domestic goods, however. Workshops and small factories began to replace individual master craftsmen in furniture manufacture. By employing semi-skilled and apprentice workers, rather than fully qualified craftsmen, and training them in particular procedures such as lathe-turning, entrepreneurs found that they could speed up production economically. Further innovations included the greater use of standard patterns and catalogues of designs; this enabled a greater specialization of machinery and labour, further cutting costs. This tendency was helped by – and in fact itself encouraged – the gradual simplification of designs, and the move away from intricate, labour-intensive pattern and applied ornament on contemporary furniture.

A very striking social development of early eighteenth century Austria, Prussia and southern Germany, was the emergence of a large, economically powerful middle class. It was this group in particular who determined what was to become the Biedermeier style; Biedermeier is often actually described as a bourgeois style, created by the bourgeois craftsman for the bourgeois client. The new commercial self-confidence of the middle classes, and their independence from the Aristocracy, led to greater assertiveness in matters of taste and style. Court fashions ceased to be the absolute hub of taste, and the merchants and professional classes felt able to choose furniture and interior decorations which better suited their own way of life, rather than attempting to ape their social superiors. In fact, a paradoxical situation resulted, in which Biedermeier styles of furniture and interior design were enthusiastically adopted by the upper classes. Even the work of Josef Danhauser's trading emporium – which had, more than any other supplier, broken the mould of aristocratic patronage of the crafts – found its way into such exclusive environments as Archduke Carl's residence, Schloß Weilburg, in Baden. It was also the direct support of Prince Metternich himself that had brought Michael Thonet to Vienna to experiment with his laminated beech veneer, a technique which eventually would turn mainstream furniture-making away from crafts and towards industry for ever.

The new class of middle class customer had more income available for spending on non-essential and luxury items than his eighteenth century counterpart; life had become less a struggle for survival, and more a quest for comfort. This is not to say that equality and contentment

ABOVE: A fallfront secretaire. The complex inlays, marquetry and gilt mounts on earlier pieces have been superseded by simpler surface treatments. Larger single pieces of veneer became more widely used throughout the period, since with the invention of veneer cutting machines it became a much less costly material.

reigned supreme, however. The situation of the poor – whether urban or rural – barely changed at all, either for better or for worse, during these three decades. In fact, in the gradual transition from a craft to a modern industrial system, many of the less talented and enterprising artisans suffered a decline in their traditional status and standard of living. In fairness, though, it must be said that a larger proportion of the population were now able to share in the luxuries that had previously been the preserve of a tiny elite.

THE MARCH REVOLUTION

BELOW: A sofa in birchwood, with inlays of rosewood and satinwood, Swedish c1820–30. The back features depictions of classical figures.

The authorities had sown the wind with their attempts to smother the populace with censorship and restriction, and they finally reaped the the whirlwind in the tumultuous events of 1848. The middle classes, at first happy to be free from the threat of war, were becoming dissatisfied with the cumbersome bureaucracy of the state, which was impeding

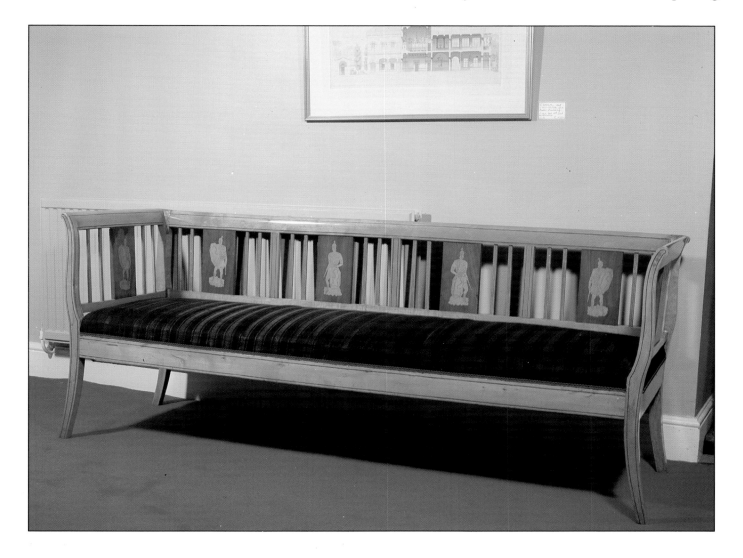

trade, and there were growing demands for a constitution. The calls for free speech and an end to censorship were at first voiced mostly by the students; but after the army used force to disperse the Viennese crowds who had gathered to hear addresses criticizing the government, support for the protest quickly gathered strength. A popular wave of discontent, hot on the heels of the abdication of King Louis Philippe in France and the founding of the Second Republic there, culminated in riots on the streets of Vienna. Unrest quickly spread to the suburbs and other cities in the Austrian Empire. This situation was mirrored in the German Confederacy nations; here it was given added impetus by the bitterness and suffering caused by a poor harvest and subsequent famine in 1846. Events progressed to such a degree that Emperor Ferdinand I (1793–1875), who had come to the throne on Francis I's death 13 years previously, was forced to abdicate, and was succeeded by the eighteen-year-old Franz Josef I (1830–1916). This was start of a new era in the politics of the region, one which finally came to a close with the outbreak of World War I. Metternich, who in the mean time had adopted the title Chancellor, fled to exile in Britain, since it was he who was most strongly associated with the unpopular measures; among the populace he had earned himself the nickname *Fürst von Mitternacht* (Prince of Midnight).

The abrupt changes in the politics of the Austrian Empire, which followed the 1848 uprisings and marked a clear conclusion to the Pre-March period, are often taken as the beginning of the end of the Biedermeier style in art and design. In truth, Biedermeier in its purest form had been in a long decline over the previous decade, particularly in the field of furniture and interior decoration. The arrival of Historicism and the 'Second Rococo', or Rococo revival in the 1830s, had already begun to dilute the character of Biedermeier. Historicism as a style dictated an eclectic approach to design; versions of Gothic, Renaissance and Baroque styles were all regarded as viable alternatives, depending on the function of the room to be furnished. Additionally, the process of industrialization, which had been gathering pace throughout the first half of the eighteenth century, was beginning to change fundamentally the cabinet-making and textiles industries. Machinery such as the Jacquard loom, which had arrived in Austria in as early as 1816, and woodworking machinery, including the power-driven circular saw, which arrived two years later, were bringing with them new possibilities and new requirements in design.

THREE

FURNITURE IN THE BIEDERMEIER PERIOD

Perhaps the best known and most sought-after manifestations of the Biedermeier aesthetic today are its remarkable pieces of furniture of all types. Indeed, the term itself is often taken to be synonymous with the calm simplicity and balance which is characteristic of the furniture design of the period. There is however a lingering uncertainty in many peoples' minds as to precisely what constitutes the Biedermeier style in furniture design; this is not helped by the differing views held by historians on the particular characteristics of the style, and on the chronological and geographical limits to the term. The style of the furniture is often described with the catch-all term neo-Classicism. Although this is strictly speaking correct, it is rather vague, since this also refers to the preceding and very different Louis Seise and Empire styles. Generally speaking, Biedermeier furniture can be described as that produced in Austria, and the German Confederation, in the late neo-Classical period of around 1810 to 1830, and in the transitional period to Historicism from around 1830 to 1850. At this point, a brief explanation of these historical terms would be helpful.

Neo-Classicism as a style in furniture, interior design, architecture and art was created as a reaction to what were seen as the excesses of the

Rococo fashion. Rococo, a predominantly French style of the early eighteenth century, is characterized by a profusion of extravagantly embellished forms, incorporating figurative motifs such as fruit and shells, as well as symbolic motifs such as scrolls and cartouches, all executed with an emphasis on the skill and artistry of the craftsman. Neo-Classicism, on the other hand, called for a return to the models provided by ancient Greek and Roman architecture: by contrast with Rococo, it embraced symmetry, relative simplicity, regular geometric shapes and forms, and a vocabulary of elements which imitated the architectural features of classical buildings. Pediments, columns, plinths, and pilasters all found their way in miniature on to cabinet-work, as did lyre-forms, scrolls, volutes and friezes. Louis Seise, Empire and Biedermeier are all manifestations of the Neo-classical tendency, and are generally used when referring specifically to furnishing and interior design, rather than contemporary culture in the main. The Louis Seise style, which as its name suggests originated in pre-revolutionary France, covered the last three decades of the eighteenth century, and was succeeded by the Empire

BELOW: A sofa, German or Scandinavian, c1820. Still heavily influenced by Rococo furniture, this piece nonetheless displays the characteristic shell-like form for Biedermeier sofas. The upholstery is absolutely typical of Biedermeier fabrics.

RIGHT: A secretaire, north German, early 19th century. The inlay, together with the overall symmetry and precision, mark this piece out clearly as part of the move away from Rococo. Typically, the brass mounts are simple and understated.

RIGHT: Secretaire in pearwood, central German, c1830. The scrolls on this piece show the trend towards large, simplified decoration, as do the unadorned columns which flank the main body.

style – the 'Empire' being that of Napoleon – in the first decade-and-a-half of the nineteenth century.

Historicism, which began to dilute 'pure' Biedermeier from around 1830 onwards, was in fact an eclectic fashion; one which drew on various past styles to create an aesthetic suitable to the environment in question. Instead of a single, unifying style from which to work, designers and craftsmen had a new plurality of choice. Different rooms in the same building might be designed in different manners, according to their function. The Gothic Revival fashion, for instance, which was particularly popular in England, and which took its cues from medieval religious architecture, might stand cheek-by-jowl with the 'Second Rococo', the revival of interest in the furnishing style of the previous century.

The sheer range of types and styles of Biedermeier furniture is astonishing. It is therefore difficult to speak of a single definitive set of characteristics as such, due to the diversity of influences and sources, although some historians have in the past attempted to constrain the use of the term to more rigid definitions. An important factor to bear in mind at all times is that the historical backdrop to the style was a shifting one; developments in technology, politics and art throughout the period all continually affected tastes in furniture and distinguished it from it predecessors to a greater or lesser extent. The increasing industrialization of the furniture making trade during this period, for instance, saw the beginnings of modern factory production in what had previously been a traditional craft. Although there was no real mass production of pieces in the modern sense of the term, entrepreneurs such as Josef Danhauser were heavily involved in batch production, or worked to pattern books which offered variations on a basic theme.

As well as changes in the structure and working practices of the furniture making industry, the introduction of new manufacturing techniques and materials were beginning to influence the design of the objects. One designer in particular, Michael Thonet, pioneered a new type of furniture which was economical and light, and at the same time robust and stylish. His bentwood furniture, made of laminated strips of beech veneer, brought with it the prospect of standard patterns, using interchangeable parts. (The continuing success of his innovation is in itself a tribute to it.) The architect Karl Friedrich Schinkel likewise helped popularize the use of cast iron as a material in furniture manufacture with his chairs and tables assembled in sections.

The rise of the 'private citizen', cocooned in his own world of domesticity and the family, can be seen as a major influence on the development of furniture in the Biedermeier era. The relative stability of politics and society in the Austrian Empire, together with gradually increasing standards of living and strict curbs on political activity, tended to promote an introspective and insular attitude among the middle classes, encouraging the active citizen to turn his efforts towards building a home rather than a nation. Patterns of life were also changing, with increasing urban populations and a greater density of housing, together with a generally higher level of ownership of furniture. This brought about a vogue for dual-purpose and space-saving pieces, such as secretaires and folding tables. Secretaires in particular appear to have found a ready market, and were a speciality of Biedermeier craftsmen. The usual drop-front design provided a worktop for writing or domestic crafts, and an abundance of storage space in the form of pigeon-holes and drawers, all in a compact and neat unit. Furthermore, when closed, not only would it give over much-needed space, but it could also be transformed in its outward appearance, from that of an essentially functional bureau, to a display object. This versatility was becoming increasingly desirable, as increasing pressure on living space meant that the same room might be used both for evenings with the family, and for entertaining guests.

ABOVE: A secretaire in mahogany, Berlin, c1820. The choice of mahogany, and the high standard of craftsmanship, distinguishes this piece as an expensive commission. The Classical architecture metaphor is most clearly apparent from the columns with their acanthus leaf and scoll capitals, and from the triangular pediment supported by the upper six columns.

RIGHT: The same secretaire open, revealing two typically bold landscape panels and an elaborate mirrored 'temple' in miniature at the centre. Even with this level of expense, however, the Biedermeier penchant for practicality is obvious in the fallfront design. which is essentially functional.

VIENNESE FURNITURE-MAKERS

Biedermeier furniture, as with so many other manifestations of the style, originated in Vienna. With the routes of communications opened up for imports and information on the latest styles from France and England after the cessation of hostilities in 1815, it became a Mecca for journeymen cabinet makers, especially those from the German states. The apprenticeship system of the time required the would-be cabinet-maker to train for three or four years with a Master cabinet-maker, and then to travel for some years before undertaking his 'masterpiece', which would demonstrate his skills of design and execution, and would finally enable him to set up shop as a master himself. The existence of this group of journeymen encouraged a mobility of ideas and talent in the trade, and ensured that even many of the provincial craftsmen had access to news of the latest fashions.

Vienna was also one of the richest social and cultural centres in the region, and presented a lucrative market for provincial and rural artisans. As early as 1816, 875 independent master cabinet makers were employed in the city; by 1823, this number had risen to 951. The authorities were keen to promote trade in the city; to this end, they established a technical college, the *Wiener Polytechnische Institut,* in 1815. This was later augmented by the efforts of several private drawing schools, including that of the Prussian-born Karl Schmidt, a respected architect and tutor, who had worked as a journeyman cabinet-maker in Prague before studying at the Academy of Fine Arts in Vienna from 1826 to 1830. The quality and esteem in which Biedermeier Vienna's furniture crafts were held had been boosted by the establishment of the *National-Fabriksproduktenkabinett* (the National Factory Products Cabinet) in 1807, which was later housed in the Polytechnic Institute. This was a collection of 'ideal' craft objects, intended to encourage excellence in all branches of

handwork. By 1829, the collection numbered some 18,000 items, including contributions from the state-run porcelain factory. Even the supplementary collection of tools ran to 3,000 articles. Further endeavours by the Viennese authorities to advertise the skills of the city's craftsmen came in 1835, with the first *Allgemeine Österreichische Gewerbs-Produkten-Ausstellung* (General Austrian Craft Products Exhibition), followed by a second in 1839 and a third in 1845.

Vienna had established its pre-eminence in cabinet making in the preceding Empire Style period, and some of the characteristic elements of Biedermeier hark back to this time. In early Viennese Biedermeier furniture, especially the more expensive and exclusive pieces, there are clear debts to French Rococo; bronze mounts, both gilt and patinated, and asymmetrical figurative ornament feature to some extent, but not in the extravagant measures typical of French work of the time. The French influence is also apparent in the names used to describe contemporary

furniture types: a large comfortable armchair was described as a *Fauteuil*, and a simple chair as a *Chaise*. The work of the cabinet-maker Benedikt Holl (*c*1753–1833) is typical of this early period; although little is known about him, save that he was born in Ellwangen (Germany), and was active in Vienna from at least 1796, it seems that he supplied pieces such as ladies' writing tables which were of unusually fine quality. His work exhibits clear elements of the Empire style, including its bronze mounts and decorative inlays, although it also contains an unmistakable move towards the closer integration of decoration and structure which distinguishes the Biedermeier style from its predecessors. Holl may have been catering to a traditional and even slightly anachronistic market, in the higher echelons of society; one which still demanded expensive embellishment and ostentatious workmanship.

As well as the French influence, English furniture designs and manufacturing techniques were highly regarded by craftsmen in the Pre-March period, particularly after the lifting of Napoleon's trade ban of 1806 and the easing of trade restrictions imposed by both the authorities and the trade guilds. The introduction of specialized machinery and factory labour, which was already heralding the onset of the industrial revolution in Britain, was to become a model for the Austrian and German furniture trades to follow in subsequent years. Certain types of furniture, such as the *Globustisch,* or spherical table, which in fact is more a cabinet than a table, were copied almost without deviation from the English pattern books. The design had been patented in England in 1806, and was often executed by Viennese cabinet-makers as a work table, with storage for items such as needlework. Its success as a piece, both aesthetically and functionally, depended very much on the skill of the individual craftsman; the upper half of the globe had to be very accurately constructed, in order that it could pivot back and down to nest in the lower half. Thomas Sheraton's (1751–1806) important book, published in London in parts around 1791 to 1793, and titled *The Cabinet-Maker and Upholsterer's Drawing Book,* was translated into German and published in Leipzig in 1794. It contained instruction on drawing and furniture design which had a demonstrable effect on craftsmen in the Austrian Empire for the next two decades. Sheraton's work was in the vein of the neo-Classicism that had influenced Biedermeier; both names, however, have come to be associated with distinctive styles, separate from the neo-Classical mainstream.

LEFT: A secretaire in mahogany. The bold simplicity of the form of this piece is one of the hallmarks of the Biedermeier style.

BELOW: A sofa in birchwood with satin inlay, Danish, c1820. The lyre form has been adapted and stylized to a great degree in this piece, but is still discernable in the form of the arms, which trace a graceful S-shape terminated by a scroll.

Certain formal elements in Biedermeier – particularly the decorative ones, such as scrolls, columns and pediments – were clearly adopted wholesale from the vocabulary of neo-Classicism. The important difference was that whereas previously these had been applied as superficial ornament, in Biedermeier they became increasingly integrated into the design and the structure of the piece. Their role became more substantial, and their scale grew, in proportion to the rest of the piece. A good example of this tendency is the lyre-form. A lyre is a harp-like instrument, featuring two symmetrical, curved uprights; as a decorative motif, it had emerged in the furniture of the earlier Empire Style. In Biedermeier furniture, it moved from the realm of ornament to that of structure, becoming more solid and three-dimensional in the process. It is a common pattern for table and cabinet legs and chair-backs, and can occasionally be seen expressed in the form of an entire object, such as a secretaire. Similarly, volutes – the spiral scrolls which had been borrowed from the capitals of classical Ionic and Corinthian columns – came to serve functional purposes, as feet for cupboards and commodes, or as visual and structural links between horizontal and vertical planes. These motifs increased in scale, at the same time reducing in number and complexity, throughout the Biedermeier era, culminating in around 1830 with the characteristic, unfussy simplicity which has become so closely associated with the style.

Craftsmen of the Biedermeier era generally favoured traditional materials for furniture construction, with the obvious exception of Thonet's bentwood and laminated woods. This special case apart, cabinet-makers used walnut and cherry woods in both their solid forms (for chairs), and veneer forms (for secretaires, cabinets and other pieces). Mahogany, because of its relative cost, tended to be reserved for only the more expensive commissioned pieces. With the increasing use of wood stains, though, it became possible to imitate the more exotic woods like mahogany. Pear wood, when dyed black, provided a reasonably-priced substitute for ebony, and was often used to pick out decorative features such as columns and beadings. Maple – inlaid, or in bird's eye veneer – is also a sign of a more expensive piece. Other solid woods and veneers, including birch, beech, oak, ash, and yew, make sporadic appearances in the furniture of the period. Work in pen and ink occasionally took the place of time-consuming marquetry, although surface pattern such as this declined during the mid 1820s. Further decoration

RIGHT, INSET: A side chair in pearwood, central German, early 19th century. This piece is virtually unadorned, save for the palmette motif in the back, which could be achieved relatively easily with a fret saw. Such furniture lent itself well to being manufactured in batches, by semi-skilled artisans in small workshops. The upholstery fabric is typical of the period.

RIGHT: A chair in fruitwood, c1820. One of a pair of chairs featuring very restrained embellishment, which is limited to a simple cut-out panel in the back featuring a stamped brass mount. Such mounts, made from thin brass sheet, or gilt carved wood, were far less expensive than the traditional cast mounts.

LEFT: A stool in fruitwood, Swedish, c1830. The flowing lines and inward-curving legs that this piece displays typify the Biedermeier feeling for simplicity and grace even in everyday furniture, and the four ebonized finials give a humorous touch.

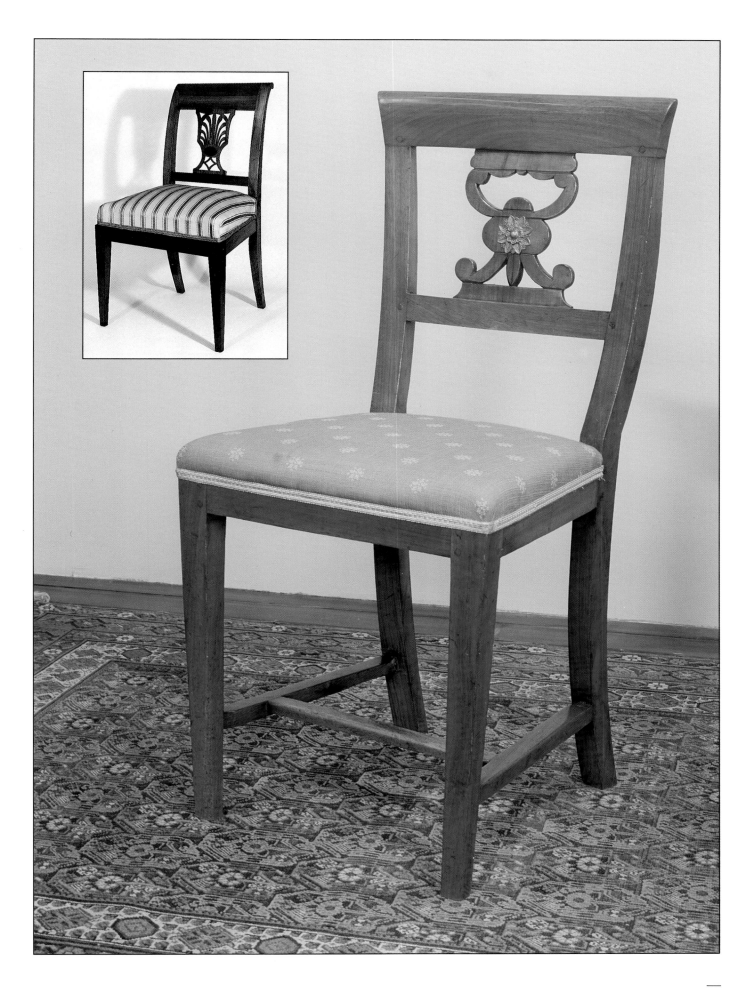

was achieved with often ingenious substitutes for the costly materials which had been popular with craftsmen in the Empire style; the gilt cast bronze mounts were approximated with thin stamped brass sheet or gilded carved wood, and the patinated bronze castings used for claw feet and caryatides were modelled in composition. The application of these types of decoration, however, had diminished by about 1825 – in Vienna, at any rate – and did not resurface until the Rococo revival a decade later. Veneers came to be used in larger single sheets, after the introduction of veneer cutting machines in the 1820s. These machines, using soaked wood, enabled a sheet of virtually any length to be peeled from the outside surface of the log, working in towards the heart wood. This technique was particularly suitable for manufacturing veneer to be used on curved surfaces, such as spheres and domes, since it was more elastic and flexible and therefore easier to work with, than conventional veneers.

In some types of furniture, such as sofas, the woodwork played second fiddle to the upholstery, especially towards the later part of the era. Although because of its fragile nature, very little of the original soft

ABOVE: A spitoon in maple veneer, Viennese, early 19th century. For all its refinement and culture, customs in Beidermeier Vienna were nonetheless quite different to those today, and spitoons were not an uncommon sight.

furnishing survives from the age of Biedermeier, contemporary records and catalogues show that great care and attention were lavished on chair and settee upholstery. Designs from the Josef Danhauser furniture factory illustrate pieces which are almost entirely covered with cushions and drapery, reflecting the fashion for elaborate draped curtains and wall hangings in interior design. The same source also gives examples of the *Couvertrahmen*, a traditional upholstered wooden frame which covered the bed and bed-clothes, enabling the bedroom to be used as a living room in the day time. This again typifies the way in which Biedermeier furniture was attuned to the functional, everyday requirements of the middle classes, rather than being aimed towards the desire to display the wealth and opulence of the aristocracy that had so deeply affected Empire and Rococo designs. It is significant that the style

BOTTOM LEFT: A small table, Viennese, early 19th century. The geometric simplicity of this piece calls to mind the Art Deco furniture of a century later.

BELOW: A sofa in mahogany, Viennese, early 19th century. The front 'legs' – actually a single piece – are in the form of a highly stylized scroll.

ABOVE: *A plant stand, with ebonized décor.*

RIGHT: *A secretaire in mahogany, with gilt mounts. This design follows a well-established pattern for such furniture, borrowing as it does from the vocabulary of neo-Classical architecture, with columns, capitals and pediment.*

ABOVE: A commode in walnut,
with ebonized columns terminated
with brass capitals.

should place such a premium on upholstery and drapery, the aspects of furniture which are most directly concerned with comfort, and it can have been no coincidence that sprung upholstery was first patented in Vienna in this period.

JOSEF DANHAUSER

One of the single most important figures in the furniture industry in the Biedermeier era was Josef Danhauser (1780–1829). Danhauser, whose father was a sculptor, was born in Vienna, and studied at the Academy of Fine Arts there. He obtained official permission to establish a factory for the production of luxury articles in 1807, extended in 1814 to cover furniture of all descriptions. This was to become his *Etablissement für alle Gegenstände des Ameublements* (Establishment for all Objects of Furnishing), whose name, with its mixture of French and German words, illustrates the still-powerful influence of French taste in the Austrian Empire at this time. By 1808, he employed over 130 workers. His entrepreneurial flair extended well beyond the manufacture of furniture alone; in addition to marketing its own factory's output, his establishment sold a wide variety of other home furnishing goods, such as carpets, clocks, glassware and fabrics. Catalogues from his emporium show that customers could choose from a remarkable selection of tables, chairs, settees, plant stands, washstands, desks, and miscellaneous objects, all offered in a bewildering profusion of options and variations, as well as oddities such as pieces in antler (a material which enjoyed a surprisingly long-lived vogue in the period). Other unusual articles included dual-purpose pieces such as combined pipe-racks and billiard cue or rifle stands, a trait typical of Biedermeier furniture. Although it is clear by the size of this operation that it appealed successfully to a large, middle class market, Danhauser also worked for the most exclusive clients too; he produced prestige work for the Archduke Carl's palace in Vienna in 1822, and for Schloß Weilburg, Baden, near Vienna. In 1825, he moved his factory and showrooms to the Karoly Palace in Wieden, a suburb of Vienna. This enabled him to display his wares in an affluent and impressive environment, as well as having space on the state for spacious and well-equipped carpentry workshops, a foundry, and gilding workshops. His death in 1829 spelt trouble for the business fortunes of the company; it struggled on, however, for another decade, before it finally ceased trading in 1839. Danhauser can be seen as the spirit of Biedermeier personified; his commercial shrewdness and diligence, and the confidence in middle class tastes that many of his pieces display, perfectly epitomize the social and cultural aspirations of his peers. Despite his prolific output, relatively few pieces survive that can be positively identified as being from his factory, apart from those pieces commissioned for Schloß Weilburg. There is however a wealth of contemporary literature and illustrative material which shows the imaginative use of form that characterizes his work. Drawings from his factory show a vast range of types and styles; over 2,500 individual designs are illustrated. These provide a measure of the degree of stylistic change in the Viennese furniture market over the years; the way in which, for example, the use of gilt mounts gradually declined, until 1825, when they had all but disappeared. The drawings also demonstrate Danhauser's inventiveness in combining function – and sometimes two or three functions – with an almost humorous use of the neo-Classical vocabulary of form. His later designs are typical of what might be termed 'high' Biedermeier; the reduction of extraneous detail, and the bold use of regular geometric solids which call to mind some Art Deco furniture of the 1920s and 30s. Scrolls, in enlarged and extended forms, with flat, unadorned side faces, and simplified lyre-forms, all executed invariably in veneered wood rather than gilt bronze, are often pressed into service as structural elements such as chair-backs and sofa legs. The beauty of the grain of veneers and solid woods was allowed to stand for itself, and the complex marquetry and inlays in exotic woods was rejected. Danhauser's son, Josef Franz Danhauser (1805–45), went on to enjoy considerable success, primarily as a painter, but also as an early proponent of the Historicist style of interior design, exemplified in engravings of his sketches for furniture which appeared in 1835 and which drew on a broader range of visual sources – including Baroque, Rococo and Renaissance – than the customary Classical references.

MICHAEL THONET

Michael Thonet (1796–1871) was another Biedermeier entrepreneur whose work was to have a profound and lasting effect on furniture design and manufacture. He was born and served his apprenticeship in Boppard on the Rhine, in Central Germany, where he set up a workshop in 1819. It was here, in around 1830, that he began experimenting with thin strips of beech and walnut veneer, sandwiched together and glued to form a composite material which was versatile, inexpensive and strong. By forming this material using a combination of pressure and heat, the smooth curves so beloved of cabinet makers of the period could be achieved relatively easily. The resulting pieces were able to feature intricate curves and scrolls without waste of wood – since the material was formed rather than being carved from solid sections – and without requiring such careful attention to traditional concerns in carpentry, such as the direction of the grain. He also used solid wood, in round sections, which was similarly manipulated, and which became known as bentwood. His unique degree of success with these techniques – which were not in themselves completely novel – led to his being summoned to Vienna by Prince Metternich, where in 1842 he was granted patents on his method of laminating and forming. In the years from 1842 to 1849, he was employed by the architect Carl Leistler (1805–1857) on the decoration and fitting-out of the Liechtenstein Palace, a show case of the revival of interest in the Rococo style, and in 1849 founded his own

BELOW: A Thonet armchair, sharing many of the features of the side chair. Thonet's furniture designs were well suited to factory production methods, using jigs and patterns; his factory eventually became a huge concern, employing thousands of workers, and his chairs have become known the world over.

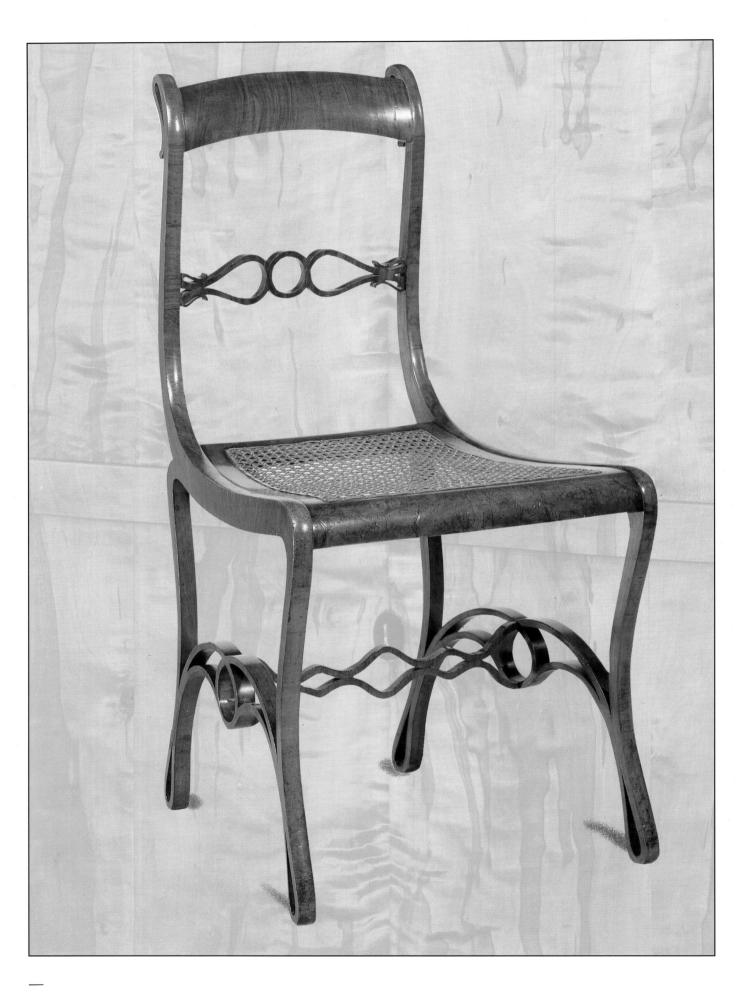

company to produce furniture to his design. Two years later, he exhibited pieces at the Great Exhibition in London, and was rewarded with a medal.

His work, initially for wealthy patrons such as Prince Liechtenstein, but later for a far broader range of customers, helped to establish a new type of light, strong, simple furniture, some of which is still available to this day. The designs produced at the factory included chairs, tables of numerous types, settees, and beds. He was uniquely able to turn the necessity of large, open curves and gradual transitions demanded by the nature of his material into an aesthetic virtue. He achieved his greatest success at the end of the Pre-March period, and indeed has been described by some historians as sounding the death knell for Biedermeier furniture styles, by ushering in a new approach to the technology of furniture manufacture. This role notwithstanding, he managed to establish one of Biedermeier's most popular and easily-recognized styles. Thonet's furniture is often associated with the arrival of Historicism and the Second Rococo, particularly bearing in mind his work on the Liechtenstein Palace. It displays even in its more complex varieties a simplicity and a preference for decorative structure, rather than simple decoration, and in this sense is typical of the idea behind Biedermeier. His firm continued to expand to the point where it became one of the world's leading furniture manufacturers, and its products were familiar all over Europe. Even after the expiry of his patents in 1869, after which point his work came to be widely copied both in Austria and abroad, the company (which had passed to his sons in 1853) continued to prosper. In 1900, the company employed 6,000 workers, making 4,000 pieces a day. Thonet's influence on subsequent designers and architects of the Modern Movement in the 1920s – most notably Le Corbusier and Marcel Breuer – is widely acknowledged.

LEFT: A chair designed by Michael Thonet, walnut and mahogany veneer with woven cane seat, Boppard am Rhein, c1835. Thonet's success in constructing 'bentwood' furniture from laminated strips of veneer, and later of solid round section wood, led to his being summoned to Vienna by Prince Metternich. His work, although often seen as heralding the onset of the 'Second Rococo', epitomises the Biedermeier concerns for function, economy and simplicity.

KARL FRIEDRICH SCHINKEL

The second centre of the Biedermeier style, after Vienna, was without doubt Berlin, home of the Prussian architect, painter, theatrical and furniture designer Karl Friedrich Schinkel (1781–1841). Schinkel was born in Neurippin, and moved to Berlin in 1794. Once there, he fell

under the spell of the architect Friedrich Gilly (1772–1800), and studied under his father David Gilly (1748–1808). He began to establish his name as an interior designer and architect in his own right in 1809, when he started work on the palace of the Prussian King, Friedrich Wilhelm III, in Berlin. This was followed by a series of commissions for the Prussian Monarchy and other prestigious works. Schinkel is perhaps best known for his neo-Classical architecture, but was also involved in the design of furniture for many of his architectural and interior design commissions. Some of his most innovative work in this sphere was created for manufacture in cast iron; he designed a range of furniture for the grounds of the Prussian Royal residences in the 1820s, some of which continued in production until the 1860s. His sources were always plural and eclectic; he had pre-empted the Historicist use of Baroque and Renaissance motifs by nearly a decade, before these became more widely applied in the region. His cast iron furniture in particular borrowed from both the locally-popular classical references, and the Gothic style which was becoming increasingly fashionable in England at the time. Surprisingly, perhaps, his work in this material was actually far in advance of that in England; he had appreciated its potential for sculptural expression in these styles well ahead of contemporary English designers. It is ironic that cast iron was a manufacturing process unlikely to have been seen as viable for furniture making by either the Ancient Greeks or the medieval craftsmen, who had provided so much of the inspiration for the visual aspects of his designs.

Karl Friedrich Schinkel was very much a versatile artistic talent, and was active in a remarkable range of disciplines – among them painting, the design of textiles and wallpaper, and metalwork in iron and precious metals. He witnessed the transition of art, architecture and crafts from the neo-Classical style to the Historicist style, while making his own significant contributions to both in the process. He therefore cannot easily be classified as belonging to a particular period or movement. His work lies on the margins of a narrow definition of 'pure' Biedermeier, in the sense that he worked to commission for aristocratic clients, as an individual with an elevated status, unlike the majority of Biedermeier craftsmen who supplied off-the-shelf pieces, usually anonymously, to their own kind, namely the middle classes. However, in stylistic terms, there are pieces of his work which typify the Biedermeier feeling for simplicity, restraint and function.

LEFT: A cast iron armchair, designed by Karl Friedrich Schinkel. This chair exhibits a number of neo-Classical motifs, including the lyre surrounded by acanthus foliage in the back, and the lions' heads which terminate the armrests. This design was without doubt one of those created for the grounds of the Prussian Royal Palaces in the 1820s, and which were produced for the general market until the 1860s.

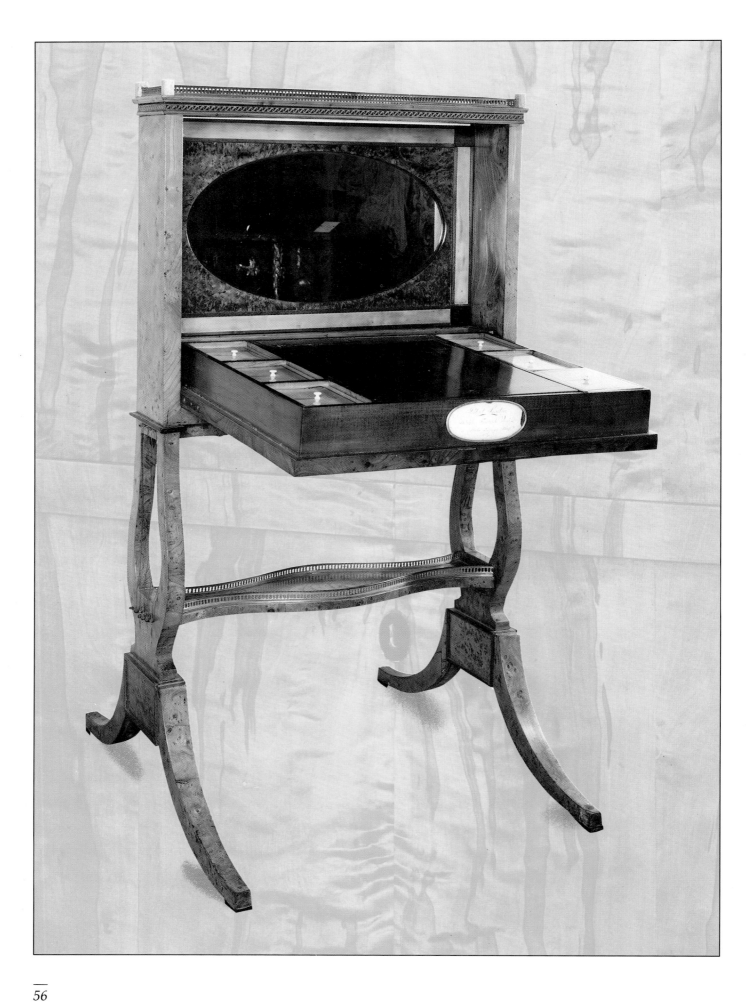

Berlin was also the home of Adolph Friedrich Voight, a cabinet-maker and designer whose work illustrates the influence exerted by both Viennese Biedermeier and English styles on the Prussian furniture crafts. He is credited with the design and manufacture of one of the earliest 'Patent Secretaires', a kind of light desk, whose top could be dropped down to form a screen, and a type of furniture which was widely copied in the later Biedermeier era. He attempted to take out a patent on the design, although it was in fact very closely copied from a design by Thomas Sheraton, the Screen Writing Table, which had appeared in *The Cabinet-Maker's London Book of Prices* (one of a series of collections of designs for furniture), published in 1788. The beauty of the type, and the characteristic which no doubt endeared it so much to the Biedermeier mentality, was its versatility; within very compact overall dimensions, it could be used as a writing desk, a sewing table, or as a bedroom table, and in its closed form could further serve as a fire screen, or be pushed back to a wall. Voight, another craftsman about whom very little else is known, was active in Berlin during the period from 1810 to 1826, when he exhibited frequently at exhibitions of crafts and industry in the city.

LEFT: A patent secretaire, made by Adolph Friedrich Voight in Berlin, c1805. Voight attempted to patent this pattern, although he had clearly based it on a Sheraton design published at the end of the previous century.

ABOVE: The same Voight secretaire closed. The versatility of this type of piece – which could serve as a desk, or be used as a screen – appealed to Biedermeier citizens, as a gradual drift towards the cities put greater pressure on living space. Note the brass wire strings in the lyre-form legs.

THE END OF THE BIEDERMEIER ERA

Some historians have argued that the end of the Biedermeier period coincided with the rise of Historicism from around 1830 onwards. This would mean that the label covers a fifteen-year duration, whose start is taken as being the Congress of Vienna, but whose end is rather more vague when defined in terms of trends in furniture design, and furthermore cannot be linked to any external political or cultural change. It is not surprising therefore to find that most people interested in the field – be they collectors, curators of museums, or academics – accept a much broader definition, which extends up to the March Revolution of 1848. Pioneering work such as that of Karl Schinkel – an early convert to the Historicist style – can in any case not always be taken as indicative of taste generally; there was without any doubt at all a considerable time-lag between acceptance of his work by the Prussian monarchy, and its adoption into the mainstream of bourgeois taste. Similarly, the 'Second Rococo' held little sway over Viennese cabinet-makers until well into the 1840s. Biedermeier had established itself as an elegant, unpretentious fashion, and moreover an attitude to the design and construction of furniture. As a style, it was ideally suited to the lives and aspirations of its clientele, and was one which could exploit the latest manufacturing technology without losing its inherent quality or charm. This straight-forwardness and lack of unnecessary complexity has been the inspiration for generations of furniture designers since; it is only ironic that the work of these followers has to some extent eclipsed the originality of its source.

RIGHT: *A decorative mirror, mother-of-pearl with gilt mounts, attributed to Carl Schmidt. The reverse of this mirror features a gouache painting by the respected miniaturist Balthasar Wigand.*

The nadir of Biedermeier's recognition as a style of furniture with integrity and validity for the present day came shortly after its final demise, in the 1850s and 1860s. Most aspects of Pre-March culture were in the process of being discredited, and were seen as somehow embody-ing the political small-mindedness and backwardness of that era. The pace of industrialization was quickening all the time, and this produced a new and fundamentally different aesthetic in furniture design. It was not long at all, however, before Biedermeier furniture underwent a cul-tural rehabilitation, and enjoyed the first of its many revivals. The occa-sion was an exhibition on the subject of the Congress of Vienna, held by the Austrian Museum of Art and Industry, in 1896. There followed a wave of interest in the area, led by the architect Josef Hoffmann (1870–1956), and the artists and designers of the turn-of-the-century Jugendstil movement, which was the German and Austrian variant of the French Art Nouveau style. Although this heralded the birth of another new and separate style, rather than a simple revival of Biedermeier as such, there were clear influences from and debts to the furniture and other crafts of the Pre-March era.

With its re-appraisal in the early years of this century, Biedermeier furniture began to be regarded as a subject worthy of study and research. It also made the gradual transition from a source of avant garde furniture style, in the shape of Jugendstil, to a more widely recognized and appre-ciated manner of design.

B I E D E R M E I E R
C E R A M I C S   A N D   G L A S S

LEFT: A Ranftbecher *with a gilt rim and cut base, featuring an illustration with the inscription* Andenken des 21. ten Mai 1816 von deinen dich liebenden Vater (*Commemoration of the 21 May 1816, from your loving father*), *by Gottlob Samuel Mohn, 1817.*

B iedermeier crafts can be seen at perhaps their most adventurous and experimental in the ceramics and glassware that was produced in the period. During the first half of the nineteenth century, glass effectively took over the role of flamboyant, creative expression that porcelain had held for the Baroque and Rococo styles. In contrast with the style of other crafts of the time, Biedermeier glass is often extravagantly decorative and ostentatious, with intricate cutting, engraving and polishing applied to a wide variety of forms. Painting in gouache and enamels, and gilding also feature heavily on the ceramics of the period. The effect, particularly in the decorative ware for which the Austrian Empire was renowned, was of sumptuous and very visible luxury, serving as a striking counterpoint to the elegant, understated simplicity of Biedermeier furniture. The pieces which have survived the ravages of time tend to be the more highly decorative objects, which because of their nature and their high value initially were usually reserved for display or occasional use only.

Although glass had long been an important industry in several of the German-speaking states, notably Silesia, Bavaria and Thuringia, it was the province of Bohemia (the region that is now western Czechoslovakia) which was the most important centre of glass manufacture and trading in the early nineteenth century. Bohemia could lay claim to a tradition of glass production stretching back as early as the fifteenth century, due in part to its abundance of raw materials – the quartz sand, chalk and minerals – and to its extensive forests which provided potash and wood for the ovens. The power demanded by the crushing machinery and grinding and polishing tools was also well catered for by the region's many rivers and streams. As early as 1803, the value of Bohemia's raw glass manufacturing was estimated at two million guilders; the elaborate finishing processes and trade in glassware earned another six million guilders, and a total of around 40,000 people were employed in the industry. Bavaria's glass trade, by contrast, yielded just 51,000 guilders in the same period. The years following the Congress of Vienna, with their improved political and economic stability, saw a steady if unspectacular growth of the Bohemian glass industry; from 66 factories in 1804, to 78 in 1820 and 99 in 1840.

It is perhaps surprising, considering its concentration in a relatively small area, that the craftsmen of the early Biedermeier glass industry should choose to look to other countries, and previous styles, for inspiration until at least the middle of the 1820s. Many of the wares produced in the closing years of the eighteenth century, such as those illustrated in the pattern book of the Harrach factory in Neuwelt (now Harrachov-Novy Svet), tend towards the well-established Rococo style. Designs in *Milchglas* ('milk' glass; a kind of opaque white glass) often served as a base for further decoration, including painted flowers and gilding; this material became an economical substitute for the more expensive porcelain. The craft was not particularly forward looking, however, either in terms of designs, or of technical advances. England and Ireland were major influences during this early period, after Ravenscroft's addition of lead to glass in 1674, which produced a softer glass with more sparkle and clarity than had previously been possible. For a considerable period, English glass was unique and highly sought after, since no other country could offer a comparable quality. The bleak years of the Napoleonic Wars, which lasted from 1799 to the Congress of Vienna in 1815, had not helped the glass craftsmen and traders in the German-speaking countries; many factories closed down, or produced wares for the domestic market only. Austria and Bohemia in particular were cut off, both from their lucrative export markets and from new developments in taste and technology. The imposition of duties and transport restrictions which followed the wars further served to impede the industry, and it was not until the 1830s that glass manufacture re-emerged as a central part of Biedermeier commerce and culture.

THE BIEDERMEIER STYLE

It is clear from surviving examples and from pattern books that the Biedermeier glass trade was beginning to establish its own distinctive style and fashions as early as the mid-1820s. One such pattern book is that published by J. F. Römisch of Steinschönau (now Kamenicky Senov) in northern Bohemia in 1832, which illustrates hundreds of cut and painted designs. Some of these, it is true, had been adapted from late eighteenth century English styles, which had set models of simplicity particularly for practical, everyday wares; others however betray more of the elaborately decorative tendency for which Biedermeier glass became famous. All manner of glass objects were offered, including beakers, glasses for wines and liqueurs, cups and saucers (both tea and coffee were drunk from glass as well as ceramic at this time), milk and cream jugs, sugar bowls, punch bowls and cups, plates and bowls for fruit and sweets, cruet services, perfume bottles, ink bottles, candle-sticks, and flower vases in a wide range of shapes and sizes. The forms and patterns were becoming increasingly independent of French Rococo porcelain, and Biedermeier glass began to find its own way as a distinctive decorative tradition.

TECHNICAL DEVELOPMENTS

The particular way in which the glass trade was organized in Bohemia and the other German states, and its traditional working practices, help to shed some light on the design and execution of glassware in the region. The plain, undecorated and usually uncut glass pieces originated at one of the factories dotted around the region. These were expensive to establish and maintain, requiring large amounts of wood for the kilns, and high quality, pure raw materials for the glass. For this reason, many were run by aristocrats and the landed gentry: the Harrach factory in

Neuwelt, for instance, was lead by Johann Pohl, on behalf of Count Harrach, and Count Longueval of Bouquoy, who developed an opaque coloured glass, owned a factory in Georgenthal in southern Bohemia. There were also entrepreneurs such as Josef Lobmeyr, who built up a glass empire, with a shop in Vienna, a factory in Slovenia, and a glass finishing workshop near Haida; he also employed many freelance engravers, painters and cutters. Middle class merchants such as Lobmeyr

became increasingly important figures in the industry throughout the period. Much of the finishing work in the industry was undertaken by self-employed craftsmen, who for the most part worked from home, buying unadorned pieces which they then decorated and sold on to retailers. Standard patterns of ware could in this way be increased in value several fold, and could easily be tailored to local or individual preferences. Many decorative pieces were sold as souvenirs of visits to large cities such as Vienna, whose St Stephans cathedral was a popular choice of illustration. Alternatively, dedications could be engraved or painted on to pieces, which were then given as family gifts and tokens of friendship.

The impulse towards a glass design which can be said to be characteristically Biedermeier was encouraged by technical experiments in producing coloured glass, chiefly with the addition of iron, copper and chrome oxides. These experiments are in many ways the counterpart of the technological developments in the cabinet-making trade at the time.

Bouquoy's development of black *Hyalith* glass was followed by Friedrich Egermann's invention of *Lythalin* glass a decade later; these opaque materials were particularly good as a base for gilding. The intention had been to imitate the stone-like quality of contemporary English opaque glass and ceramics. Another popular technique was overlaying of coloured glass on to clear glass or opaque white glass. With subsequent cutting and polishing, complex designs could be achieved.

Graf von (Count) Longueval Bouquoy (1781-1851) was a typical aristocratic factory owner; he became the sole manufacturer of the opaque black glass Hyalith, which he had developed in 1820. He also produced a red Hyalith glass. Opaque coloured glass was not a completely new invention; its manufacture had been known in Bohemia since the previous century. The Bouquoy factory's wares were particularly successful, however, to the extent that some were sent to finishers and painters in other parts of the region, as the factory could not cope with the demand.

Friedrich Egermann (1774-1864) was another early experimenter with coloured glass. He was awarded a permit in 1828 to produce what he called Lythalin, a dark reddish-brown opaque glass, often exhibiting a marbled surface. He displayed wares alongside his rival Count Bouquoy, at the 1829 Bohemian Industrial Products Exhibition in Prague, where he described himself as being the privileged manufacturer of jewel glass and Lythalin in Blottendorf. He received silver medals for both this and his work on show at the same exhibition two years later. It is known that his products additionally appeared in the prestigious National Factory Products Cabinet. Egermann's process enabled other colours to be added to the marbling, which were then fused into the body of the glass by supplementary firing, resulting in complex and well-defined colours in a variety of hues. He was careful to keep this technique secret, and even attempted to throw his rivals off the scent by claiming it resulted from the addition of vegetable matter to the raw glass. He continued to experiment and innovate in new types of glass, introducing another version of Lythalin in 1831, and sold wares to the Harrach factory and its director Johann Pohl (1769-1850), brother of the respected glass engraver Franz Pohl (1764-1834).

Further technical developments in glass manufacture include the so-called *Überfanggläser,* the layered coloured glass which was first produced in Neuwelt and was soon after copied by other factories. It enabled selective application of colour – the thinner the layer, the lighter the colour – or an all-over layer of colour, which could then be cut and etched to reveal the clear glass underneath. This technique in particular, when combined with other forms of decoration such as gilding and painting, allowed a virtually unlimited permutation of design, and was popular until around 1850. Engraving such a piece would yield a striking effect of a white image on a coloured ground. The covering layer – or layers, since as many as four or five could be added – had to be fused on to the body of the piece in a furnace after being applied. This meant that the process could only be carried out at a factory which was large enough to support a kiln; an important point, since undecorated pieces had traditionally been sent out to independent studios for cutting, gilding and painting. A similar effect to overlaying of glass was often achieved by staining and glazing glass; this however appears to have been less prestigious, as contemporary descriptions of the former process emphasize the fact that the colours are fused into, and are therefore integral with, the surface of the piece.

The addition of uranium to glass produced a yellow-green glass which was particularly popular from the 1840s onwards. These pieces have an almost fluorescent quality in daylight. The material was invented by Josef Riedel, a glass-maker in the Isengebirge region; he named it *Annagelb* or *Annagrün,* after his wife Anna. Similar types were popular in Britain, where they were known as Canary Glass, and in France at around the same time. This was perhaps the most spectacular, but far from the only innovation in coloured glass; the Harrach factory, along with many other factories and individuals, constantly strove to produce exotic new colours in both transparent and opaque varieties.

Gradually throughout the period, a selection of forms emerged which typify Biedermeier glass. The *Pokal,* a decorative beaker or vase, is the most common subject of further finishing. In addition to the traditional simple straight-sided cylindrical glasses, which served largely as vehicles for the talents of the glass finishers, the *Ranftbecher,* a waisted glass with a heavy, notched rib at its base was a popular form; both the rim and the base were invariably gilded. Other beakers were produced with thick walls, which lent themselves to elaborate cutting and etching;

some of these feature cut lenses in their walls, which serve to magnify the painted or engraved decoration on the opposite side of the piece. Pedestal feet were popular features of bowls and goblets, and some feature fluting, facets in the form of hexagons and octagons, or petal-shaped profiles. Table centrepieces – two- or three-tiered decorative stands, on which sweets and fruit would be served after meals – and small drinking glasses with saucers are also typical, as well as covered goblets, trinket boxes and decanters.

The development of pressed glass and forms for blown glass began to make its mark, albeit at first slowly, on the Austrian and German glass trade. The use of dampened wooden moulds for forming blown glass was not new; it had been common when producing pieces in batches. The technique was developed further however into a factory process using more durable metal moulds in America in the early eighteenth century, culminating in 1827 with the introduction of pressed glass. In this process, the glass is heated to a semi-molten state, and is then pressed into a negative mould, the interior of which can feature quite complex decoration. The early examples of this type imitate closely the models of English cut glass of the time, the difference being that, having invested in a single mould, hundreds or thousands of identical, elaborate articles could be produced quickly and cheaply.

Traditionally, such decoration had been reserved for the more expensive and exclusive pieces; but the pressed glass process brought the appearance of cut glass to wares of all price levels. The Austrian and Bohemian factories were relatively slow to take up the new process, however. The entrepreneur Franz Steigerwald is known to have imported equipment for pressed glass manufacture at his factory in Theresienthal as early as 1836, but nothing is known of his success with the technique; certainly none of these wares were exhibited at the Bohemian industrial exhibitions of the time. Only in the subsequent decades did pressed glass begin to have a very significant place in the glass trade, apart from the activities of Josef Lobmeyr, a glass dealer and factory owner who achieved such a degree of success with his sales of imported French wares that he decided to start producing it himself. Most of the Bohemian factories, realizing that they had fallen behind the French and British in this particular area, elected to stick with the more traditional types of glass manufacture and glass finishing, as well as the speciality of coloured glass production.

Individual dealers exercised a surprising degree of influence on tastes in the glass trade. Because of the diverse nature of the industry, and the fact that an individual piece might pass through the hands of various glass cutters, engravers and painters after it had left the factory, it was the traders who were best placed to predict changes in fashion. One of the best-known dealers, Franz Steigerwald, sold pieces by many of the finest engravers in Bohemia in his shop in Würzburg; he eventually even opened a shop in England, in around 1850.

A particular speciality of Bohemian glass was its rich decoration, which often incorporated gilding, engraving and painting all in the same piece. Engravers such as Dominik Biemann, August Böhm and Anton Pelikan, were much in demand; Biemann was commissioned to produce portraits on glass of some of the most important aristocrats of the Austrian Empire. Glass painters, such as Samuel Mohn and his son Gottlob Samuel Mohn, and Anton Kothgasser, specialized in flowers, sentimental tableaux and tokens of love and friendship, and views of cities such as Vienna, executed with technical virtuosity in gouache and enamels.

GLASS ENGRAVERS

Dominik Biemann (1800-1857) is widely regarded as having been one of the very best engravers active in Bohemia in the Biedermeier era. He was born in Neuwelt, the son of a mould-maker at the Harrach glassworks. From 1825, he worked in the spa town of Franzensbad, creating portraits of the wealthy visitors to commission during the peak season, and it is for these pieces that he is best known. He attended the Academy of Fine Arts in Prague two years later, and subsequently was granted permission to set up an engraving studio there. Biemann exhibited his work at the Prague Industrial Exhibitions of 1829 and 1831, including portraits of the philosopher and poet Goethe, Napoleon, and Emperor Franz I. His reputation as a first-class engraver of both portraits and other subjects, such as hunting scenes and depictions of historical subjects, had spread to Berlin by 1835, when he was commissioned to produce portraits of the Prussian Royal Family. He supplied pieces to Franz Steigerwald (1789-c1865), the entrepreneur for whom he had been working since 1828. It seems that Biemann's business acumen was not

up to the superlative standard of his engraving, however; he was poorly paid for his work for Steigerwald, and his attempts to set up shop in Vienna in 1839 were not met with great success. Many pieces known to have been supplied by Steigerwald's shop in Würzburg are strongly suspected to be Biemann's work, although they, unlike his Franzensbad commissions and his other wares, are unsigned. He was without doubt a perfectionist, and at heart an artist rather than a businessman; only this could account for his obsessive attention to the finest detail, and his technical mastery. Towards the end of his life, this attitude served him badly; afflicted by mercury poisoning from the gilding process, he became ill and unable to work.

August Böhm (1812-1890) and Franz Anton Pelikan (1786-1858) are the two other glass engravers active at this time whose work is of the highest standard. Pelikan's work was displayed at the Prague Industrial Exhibition in 1831; it was also sold by one of the leading glass dealers in the region, Bienert in Teplice, who contributed to the *National-Fabrik-produktenkabinett* in Vienna. Only one of Pelikan's signed pieces survives, but several other unsigned works, including decorative vases with hunting scenes, have been attributed to him, on the basis of detailed analysis of the engraving technique and subject matter. Böhm specialized in depictions of battles (a popular choice of subject among glass engravers of the time), historical scenes based on paintings, and portraits.

GLASS PAINTERS

Samuel Mohn (1762-1815) was originally a porcelain painter, who began to experiment with transparent enamel painting on glass around 1806, the art of which he claimed to have re-discovered after it had been long forgotten. He sent an example of his work, a painted decorative vase, to the Prussian Queen Louise; this appears to have been well received, and Mohn enjoyed further Royal patronage in the following years. Mohn's work is by far the best known of this type of glass decoration. His favourite subjects were views of landmarks and cities, including the Brandenburger Gate in Berlin, and his home town of Dresden, where he had moved from Leipzig in 1809. Unlike his contemporary in the field of glass engraving, Dominik Biemann, Mohn in addition to being a first-rate craftsman, was an astute entrepreneur and businessman, who ran a

RIGHT: Three examples of the Ranftbecher. *Left to right: an anonymous vase with a playing card illustration; a vase attributed to Anton Kothgasser with a topographical view inscribed* Frauenthor a Baden; *and a view inscribed* La cathédrale de St Etienne à Vienne, *also attributed to Kothgasser. The fact that the inscription is in French gives some indication of Vienna's importance as a tourist town.*

successful and highly productive glass painting studio employing several other painters; this is evidenced by the appearance of additional signatures on his pieces. He produced a range of enamel-painted wares to suit all pockets, from the simple illustrations of butterflies and flowers up to elaborate panoramic views and landscapes, occasionally incorporating text in the form of inscriptions. Mohn's son, Gottlob Samuel Mohn (1789-1825), attended the Academy of Fine Arts in Dresden, before continuing his father's success with this technique, moving to Vienna in 1811 and producing work in a similar vein. The secret of the success of their work lay in its uniqueness – few if any other glass painters had the technical knowledge of the ingredients and firing processes needed to produce vivid, translucent colours on glass reliably. Such was Gottlob Samuel Mohn's reputation, that he was able to move in elevated social circles, and was commissioned to create paintings for the windows of Schloß Laxenburg in 1813.

The younger Mohn appears to have worked at least for a short period alongside his main rival in Vienna, Anton Kothgasser (1769–1851). Kothgasser had studied at the Academy of Fine Arts there from 1781, and subsequently worked as a painter and gilder at the Vienna Porcelain Factory. He produced his first painted glasses around 1812, while still being employed by the factory; by 1816, however, he left, his freelance

Pieces from the Vienna Porcelain Factory, featuring a hand-painted vine leaf motif in green on a white glaze ground, executed in 1822. RIGHT: A coffee or chocolate pot, a tea pot and a cup and saucer.

BELOW: Another piece from the Vienna Porcelain Factory, a fruit bowl.

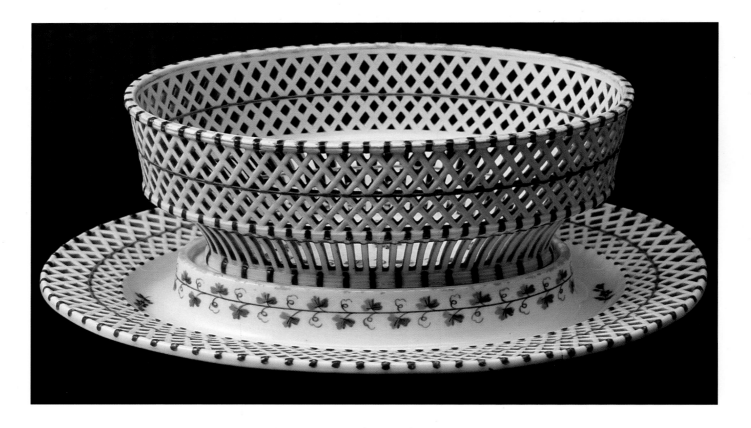

work having taken over completely. His pieces use both translucent and solid enamels, and he favoured either straight-sided cylindrical glasses, or the so-called *Ranftbecher*, a slightly waisted beaker with a heavy, cut base, and a gilded rim. A peculiarity of his work is that the illustration is invariably enclosed within a silver border; the subjects tend towards the consistently-popular city views, flowers and plants, and portraits, as well as a number of views of the St Stephans cathedral in Vienna. His illustrations use both clear and white backgrounds. In 1839 he exhibited wares from his workshop at the second General Austrian Craft Products Exhibition. Kothgasser sold many of his pieces through a business arrangement with Leopold Schadlbauer, a retailer who owned a shop on the Stephansplatz in Vienna.

RIGHT: Painted porcelain ware from the Viennese Porcelain Factory, c1825.

BIEDERMEIER PORCELAIN

Porcelain was to some extent overshadowed by the more spectacular developments in glass manufacture and painting; indeed, both Samuel Mohn and his son Gottlob Samuel Mohn came to the latter field from the discipline of porcelain painting. Emphasis, as with the glassware of the period, was very much on decoration and surface pattern, rather than

LEFT: A cup and saucer with a gilt rim and a portrait of Emperor Francis I, Vienna Porcelain Factory, 1849.

TOP, ABOVE & OPPOSITE PAGE:
Three illustrations from the Royal
Imperial Porcelain Factory,
gouache on paper, signed Johann
Garo, Friedrich Gesswald, and
Josef Wundsam, dated 1819
and 1820.

form, and again like glassware, a range of levels of decoration was available to suit a wide variety of pockets and tastes. Designs for porcelain forms were very much influenced by classical patterns; urns and amphora-like forms crop up frequently in the commissioned wares.

One of the central influences on Biedermeier porcelain was the Royal Imperial Porcelain Factory in Vienna; this had been established a century previously, in 1718, and had been taken over by the Austrian Treasury in 1744. It was highly regarded for its decorative wares, including ornamental plates illustrated with the traditional views of the city, copies of well-known paintings, and allegorical or genre scenes; these themes were also carried over to cups and saucers. Gilding was extremely popular, especially on rims, edges and handles, and extending to the interior of the more expensive pieces. Although few if any major technological breakthroughs were made in the ceramics industry in the region at this time, new working practices were beginning to have a major effect on the way in which the Royal Imperial Porcelain Factory operated. The director of the factory from 1805 to 1827, Matthias Niedermayer, continued the rigid system of narrow specialization among the 500 strong workforce that had been instituted under his predecessor, Conrad Sögel von Sorgenthal. A consistently high standard of work was ensured by dividing the painters into sub-groups according to subject matter: landscape, portrait, flower and pattern. These artists had at their disposal a vast range of colours for the most elaborate pieces. The factory undertook all types of work, from simple single-colour designs with a flower or leaf motif and a border, at one end of the spectrum, to large, extravagantly decorated services, employing several painters simultaneously, which would be commissioned by prestigious clients at the other end. Although artists at the factory commonly imitated seventeenth-century Dutch painters such as Jan van Huysum and Rachel Ruysch, individuals including the still-life painter Josef Nigg (1782–1863) emerged as original talents, indeed, the factory actually employed respected painters in their own right. Nigg had trained at the Academy of Fine Arts in Vienna, and remained at the factory until 1848. The Porcelain factory finally ceased production in 1864, due to competition from areas of Bohemia which had naturally occurring kaolin clay and consequently lower costs.

FIVE

BIEDERMEIER ARCHITECTURE, INTERIORS AND DOMESTIC LIFE

Architecture and interior design in the Biedermeier era can be seen as being the confluence of several different strands of style. It is in this field, as much as in furniture design, that the Biedermeier ideal is expressed. The relatively rapid transition from the Court- and Aristocracy-dominated tastes of the Empire period, to a more widely-based and more democratic aesthetic in the years after the Congress of Vienna, can be seen particularly clearly in the sphere of the domestic interior, and to a slightly lesser extent, in the official and private architectural commissions of the time.

DOMESTIC ARCHITECTURE

As much as any other individual factor, it was necessity that brought about Biedermeier values and attitudes, as they are expressed in residential building. Gradual commercial growth and development, which had been gathering pace since the middle of the previous century, and had only been checked by the insecurity and austerity of the Napoleonic Wars, meant that there was an ever-increasing pressure on land in the cities. This was especially true of Vienna, where the historical fortifications had always presented a physical and political brake on expansion. This continued to be the case until 25 December 1857, when Emperor Franz Joseph I issued a decree permitting the demolition of the fortifications, allowing the further growth of the centre of the city. This year is taken by some historians as being the final end of the Biedermeier era, as far as architecture and interior design are concerned. The population of the city of Vienna grew from about 300,000 in the 1820s to around 430,000 in 1857. This influx of people, among them a sizeable proportion of well-to-do bourgeois citizens, into a geographically constrained area, created a new requirement for compact living; this imperative being reflected in both the architectural forms, and the patterns of life of the

BELOW: An adjustable-height writing desk.

inhabitants. In this sense, Biedermeier was more a frame of mind, and an attitude to life, rather than merely a superficial style, as Empire and Rococo had been.

In an unusual, although not entirely unprecedented turn of events, the upper classes – the Court, and the aristocracy who had previously dictated fashion – actually assimilated and emulated the bourgeois tastes to a remarkable degree. Even the Emperor, in the years immediately after the Congress, appears to have favoured simpler, less ornate forms of furniture and interior decoration, if contemporary reports are to be believed. Another leading member of Viennese society, Archduke Charles (1771-1847), a former military man and adversary of Napoleon at the battle of Aspern in May 1809, provides additional evidence of this tendency towards a more universal taste. He commissioned the architect who has become most closely associated with Biedermeier architecture, Josef Kornhäusel (1782–1860), to design both his city residence, the palace of Albertina, and his country retreat, Schloß Weilburg, near Baden in southern Austria. (The latter building was also extensively furnished by Josef Danhauser's factory, which, significantly, had established its considerable reputation in the first place as suppliers of off-the-shelf pieces to the bourgeoisie.) Kornhäusel trained at the Academy of Fine Arts in Vienna, and was subsequently employed by Prince Liechtenstein as his architectural director, until 1818. He was active on a range of commissions in Vienna in the 1820s, including Albertina, an inherited building which he adapted for the Archduke in the years between 1822 and 1824, and Schloß Weilburg, which he built from the ground up in the same period. In both cases, Kornhäusel was required to incorporate the traditional function of an aristocratic building – that of displaying the family wealth and splendour acquired over generations – with the new and altogether different desire for comfort and practicality. This he achieved by clearly separating the public from the private aspect of the buildings. Stylistically, the buildings feature Kornhäusel's particular interpretation of the neo-Classical vocabulary of forms. It was his ability to mesh this conventional aesthetic – in itself, far from unique to Biedermeier – with the almost prosaic attention to detail and function which characterized Biedermeier attitudes in this and other fields of creativity.

In addition to the pressure of lack of building land already mentioned, there was another influence on the architecture of the period, although this one was rather more deliberate. It will come as no surprise, bearing in mind its intervention in just about every other field of creative endeavour, that the state exercised a guiding hand on building in Vienna in the Biedermeier era. Indeed, since a licence was needed to establish even a modest-sized cabinet-making workshop, and official approval was required in advance for all published books, pamphlets, and prints, it is not surprising that the authorities should want to control very visible and permanent manifestations of individual expression such as buildings. This control was exercised in a variety of ways, some more direct than others. Religious buildings, bar Catholic ones, were required by law to be invisible from the street; hence, a synagogue, in whose design Joseph Kornhäusel was involved, had to be concealed behind another residential building. Other more benign forms of influence were exercised through the *Hofbaurat,* or Court Architectural Committee, a group established in 1809 for the purpose of leading architecture by example; it was been responsible for, among others, the design of the *Wiener Polytechnische Institut.*

It may seem strange that the authorities should fear the supposedly 'revolutionary' aspects of architecture; but this was undoubtedly the case. Historicism, which had begun to emerge in architecture rather earlier than it had in mainstream furniture design, was seen as being potentially seditious, and was clamped down on by Prince Metternich and Peter von Nobile (1774–1854), the man who Metternich had chosen to lead the architectural wing of the Academy of Fine Arts in 1818. Von Nobile's work is in many ways characteristic of the stridently formal Classicism approved of by the state, and reflected in many of its other commissions. His Temple of Theseus, situated in the Volksgarten (Public Park) and erected in the years 1819 to 1823, can be seen as being symbolic, not only of a rather obvious political allegory (the building houses Antonio Canova's sculpture of Theseus fighting the Minotaur), but also of the rigid adherence to a set of unquestioned aesthetic rules which allowed little or no personal expression on the part of the architect. The building itself was a copy of an Athenian original, albeit to a some-what more modest scale. This type of approach was further developed in other official buildings, to the extent that a kind of ruthless, austere functionalism ensued; no doubt it was more a consequence of the need for large, impressive and efficient buildings at as low a cost as reason-ably feasible, rather than the development of some new ethic of architec-tural design.

RIGHT: A fallfront secretaire with extending work surface in mahogany, Viennese, early 19th century. The arch at the centre of the interior gives a clue to the Gothic themes which became popular with the rise of the eclectic Historicist style from the 1830s onwards.

LEFT: *A commode in birchwood,
with rosewood and satinwood
inlay, Danish, c1820.*

Peter von Nobile's successor at the Academy of Fine Arts was the architect Paul Sprenger (1789-1854), a man who had been a pupil of his, and who was well versed in the officially approved doctrine of neo-Classicism. He was appointed as the professor of architecture at the Academy in 1828, and in 1842 took over the directorship of the Hofbaurat. His influence on Viennese architecture during this period was remarkable, since he lead the two institutions which directly and indirectly controlled taste and fashion in this field. A design which is typical of his copybook Classicism is the Viennese Customs Office and Provincial Revenue Administration Building, built from 1840 to 1847. Surprisingly, however, Sprenger became a convert to Historicism, shortly after this building was completed.

Changing patterns of life partly fuelled, and were partly the consequence of, changes in residential architecture in the city of Vienna and its suburbs. The most immediate effect on urban and suburban accommodation was the rise of apartment blocks. These served as townhouses for the richer middle-class inhabitants, and as year-round dwellings for the less well-off. A typical form for this type of house was a tall, several storey (commonly five or six) building, with an imposing rendered façade composed of very regularly arranged features such as doorways and windows. Symmetry was considered as being of the utmost importance; even if the actual layout and ground plan of the building were asymmetrical, the shape and distribution of the architectural elements would be so arranged as to give the illusion of balance. Ground floor façades would often be quite elaborate, with decorative mouldings, and columns with capitals and pediments, adorning the doorways. The upper floors would each have a subtly different façade treatment, usually becoming plainer towards the top, while retaining the horizontal repetition of detail. Window frames on the more ornate frontages featured arch-forms or were capped with semi-circular fanlights. Access to individual apartments were either by common halls and stairways, or by external, open landings.

INTERIOR DESIGN

The interior of the Biedermeier town house or apartment was similarly affected by the need to economize on space so far as possible. This led to some of the more remarkable pieces of furniture of the period; the obviously practical space-saving designs, such as secretaires and extend-

BELOW: The same commode, opened to reveal a writing desk with compartments for stationery. Dual-purpose furniture such as this was consistently popular in apartment rooms which were required to serve as both public and private spaces.

ing tables, were joined by improbable-looking multi-function pieces which appear in the catalogues of the Danhauser Furniture Factory. Unfortunately, none of the more outlandish examples, such as a portable washstand, have survived; indeed, it is unclear as to whether these pieces were ever in fact made and sold. By way of contrast, the patent secretaire, which had been derived very closely from a design published by Thomas Sheraton in the late eighteenth century, appears to have been a very successful and sought-after pattern; it could double as a light desk or a fire screen. Other types of furniture, such as the conventional secretaire already mentioned, and the so-called cylinder-top desk (which is similar to a roll-top desk, except that the top is constructed from a solid, cylindrical part), permitted furniture whose character was essentially functional to be disguised to some extent.

The attention in the Biedermeier interior focussed quite emphatically on the living room as the communal hub of the home. No longer was this a highly ostentatious part of the house, used only for entertaining guests and displaying wealth. It became a comfortable and versatile space; the family would spend evenings together here, reading, playing music or engaged in domestic crafts such as needlework. Its role had changed from a public, formal one to a private, informal one, but one which was nevertheless required on occasion to look smart and respectable for entertaining company. Quite apart from the fact that the bourgeoisie did not have the disposable income to support a lavish patronage of the arts and crafts, they also did not have the inclination for competitive and symbolic spending. Arrangements of furniture reflected this new, family-centred attitude; the living room was laid out according to the more complex and various functions it had to serve. The scale of interior design became more human, and less inclined toward the imposing grandness of Rococo and Empire. In an interesting counter-current to developments in contemporary furniture design, Biedermeier interiors began to embrace complexity and small details, often expressing a more personal and even sentimental approach to objects. Keepsakes, mementoes of family and friends, and souvenirs of visits to other places, such as the decorative glasses which were engraved or painted with views of landmarks, took increasing pride of place, on shelves and mantelpieces, or in display cabinets. The strict symmetry and formality of earlier room arrangements was softened considerably during the period, for practical reasons of economy of space, and for reasons of comfort.

RIGHT: A tilt top table in birchwood and mahogany, with inlays of rosewood and satinwood, and ebonized decor, Danish, c1820. Another space-saving design, the surface of tilt top table could also serve as a decorative function when not in use.

A particularly useful source of information on contemporary interiors of ordinary Biedermeier homes is provided in the form of watercolour and gouache illustrations. These pictures appealed to the middle classes, who for the most part would not have been able to afford the much more expensive oil paintings. Other sources of information are the Danhauser Factory design drawings, which are now in the collection of the Austrian Museum of Applied Arts; these give a wealth of examples of fabric patterns and arrangements of drapery.

Colours in Biedermeier interiors, like a surprising number of other historical styles, were often in what would today be regarded as bright, or even loud hues. With gradual advances in the use of pigments and dyes, stronger and more saturated colours were becoming available all

BELOW: Heinrich Krüppel: Green Room with a view onto the Veste Burglaßschlößchen at Coburg, gouache, signed and dated June 1832. Although it clearly represents an aristocratic interior rather than a bourgeois one, this picture illustrates many typical features of the Biedermeier home. The ceiling is plain white, save for a rose picked out in contrasting

the time, and they were seized upon enthusiastically by the decorators of the period. Unfortunately, because of their fragile nature, few examples of wallpapers and furnishing fabrics survive, and many of those that do have become faded and worn, retaining little of their erstwhile brilliance. To get some feeling for the popularity of very vivid colours, it is necessary to survey some of the early nineteenth century silk weavers' sample books; swatches which have been preserved here, protected from the effects of light and dust, show a remarkable selection of colour-ways and patterns.

A favourite type of pattern, for both wallpaper and printed and woven textiles, was a broad stripe, often containing a repeated motif such as a bouquet of flowers, and usually bordered by a narrower band of another colour, on a contrasting background. This has subsequently become regarded as a hallmark of the Biedermeier interior, although many other patterns were produced in addition, such as small flower repeats, and mock watered-silk prints. Neo-Classical influenced frieze designs, incorporating flowers or leaf patterns, were very common, especially just below the cornice at the top of the wall, just above the skirting board, and again (in a reduced version) around the edge of the cornice where it meets the ceiling. The same theme – either printed on paper, or stencilled directly on to the plaster – would be repeated in a circular form around the ceiling rose. As an alternative form of decoration, especially in the more expensive homes, *trompe-l'œil* mural paintings simulated plaster relief mouldings, depicting typically Classical subjects such as urns and acanthus foliage.

Ceilings, in contrast to the busy and florid wallpapers and textiles, were traditionally kept in a pale, plain colour, often white. Plaster reliefs, such as ceiling roses, cornices, and picture rails, could then be picked out in another colour. Form the 1820s onwards, there was a growing trend for drapery. This originated with the generously cut curtains, which gradually grew in scale and complexity, until they covered entire walls. These curtains were hung from rails and were usually held open with ties decorated with braid and lace, or were alternatively held open using hooks which resembled a gilded medallion on the end of a short stem. Festoon hangings were also in evidence. The vogue of draped fabrics, usually in paler colours, being used instead of wallpaper was particularly predominant in dressing rooms and ladies' bedrooms, where it spread to furniture design. Chairs and dressing tables were

colours, as is the cornice. The bold stripe pattern of the wall covering echoes similar patterns in furnishing fabrics of the time. Note also the draped curtains, and the way that they are reflected in the upholstery on the sofa against the far wall. The floorcovering is an early form of a wall-to-wall carpet, in a large geometric repeat.

fitted with matching valances, and beds were either virtually enclosed in extravagant folds of curtains, or in the more modest homes, were disguised with the traditional *Couvertrahmen,* a framed, upholstered coverlet. The catalogues of the Josef Danhauser Factory show that this phenomenon was by no means restricted to bed chambers, however: several examples of sofas and chairs which are almost entirely covered in fabric are illustrated there. This prevalence of soft furnishing created an environment which served to enhance the sensation of privacy and sumptuousness.

Floor coverings in the Biedermeier home were rather simpler and less lavish than the other furnishing fabrics. Fine parquet floors, or, in the more modest house, stained and varnished floorboards, provided a contrast with the heavy upholstery and drapery; patterned rugs and larger carpets were used under the chairs, sofas and tables. Alternatively, carpets which extended across the whole floor, from wall to wall, were laid. Darker colours were favoured for floor coverings, which featured medium-sized repeats of flowers, leaves or abstract patterns.

ABOVE: Emilius Bärentzen:
A Portrait of the Schram
Family, *oils on canvas. This painting shows a more modest Biedermeier interior; note the plain varnished floorboards, and the small rug under the table. The curtains are nonetheless carefully draped and held back, however, and the sofa is richly upholstered.*

The love of nature and all things natural was a new development in the Biedermeier era; it had its seeds in the Romantic movement in art, literature and philosophy, which had emerged in the late eighteenth century. This was a reaction against the materialism of the sciences and industry, and against the formality of neo-Classicist aesthetics in art and architecture. It can be seen as a nostalgic throw-back to the pre-industrial era, a view that holds that life was more natural and less complicated before the advent of the machine, the town, and the sciences. Whether or not this was true – an unlikely supposition in the Austrian Empire, since the majority of the population in the pre-industrial times had been rural agricultural workers, living at subsistence level – it had a profound effect on attitudes to nature in this period. The literature of the German *Sturm und Drang* writers of the 1770s, including the young Johann Wolfgang von Goethe (1749–1832), and Johann Gottfried Herder (1744–1803), as well as that of writers of other nationalities, such as Sir Walter Scott (1771–1832), created a stirring picture of a rural idyll. This was an image to which writers of the Biedermeier era, including Adalbert Stifter (1805–1868) in his novel *Der Nachsommer,* enthusiastically contributed. This influence filtered down from literature and art, through landscape architecture and garden design, to the domestic interior, where it manifested itself in rich displays of indoor plants and flowers, which were at times combined with rather unlikely pieces of furniture, such as a jardinière-cum-birdcage-cum-fish bowl stand illustrated in the Danhauser Furniture Factory catalogues. A Biedermeier living room would often house a less ambitious jardinière and a plant stand or two; caged birds were also not uncommon, adding as they did the sound of bird song to an environment, and thus evoking further the atmosphere of the countryside.

OUTDOOR LIFE

The vogue for natural things also extended outside the home. The better-off families could still afford to continue the upper class tradition of separate town and country residences, and so had little need to express their affinity for nature, but for the vast majority of the population, the countryside was becoming more and more distant. Very few houses in Vienna enjoyed the luxury of a private garden; in common with patterns of urban development in other European major cities, the move to apartment living made this impractical. The substitute adopted by the authorities was the establishment of public parks, such as the Prater and the Augarten, on the banks of the Danube. The Prater was a combination of pleasure parks, fairground sites, formal gardens and forests, which was extremely popular with the Viennese. It had previously been a hunting reserve, access to which had only been permitted to the élite aristocracy, until it was opened up to the general public by Emperor Joseph II. This original function explained the scale and the very natural-istic layout, which displayed few of the signs of having been created by man, except for the boulevards and the very numerous monuments, pavilions and cafés. The inns and taverns existed to serve the flocks of visitors who arrived in summer, for the traditional celebrations sur-rounding holy days, and in winter, for the *Fasching* carnival, a custom which survives in Austria and Germany to this day. There were also firework displays on the *Feuerwerkplatz* several times a year. The Prater was a favourite subject for artists and illustrators, who have left a rich legacy of visual records of Viennese life in the Biedermeier era, and was also described in detail as it appeared at carnival time by various con-temporary writers. The descriptions reflect a range of perceptions of the way in which the citizens used the park; some depict families out walking in a peaceful and civilized environment, or music recitals in the open air, whereas others reflect a less idealized (but probably more realistic) pic-ture of drunken ribaldry among the working classes on feast days. The Augarten, by contrast, which lay in Leopoldstadt, to the south of the old city, was a more formally laid out garden which was intersected by regular pathways. It too was taken over by the crowds during the car-nival; at other times of year, it was a popular venue for open-air concerts.

ABOVE: *An anonymous gouache painting of the coffee house in Vienna's Volksgarten, c1825.*

KARL FRIEDRICH SCHINKEL

Outside the virtual tyranny that Metternich wielded over Biedermeier architecture in the Vienna of the Austrian Empire, it was without doubt the Prussian architect Karl Friedrich Schinkel (1781–1841) who defined the most distinctive style of the period. Schinkel was educated at the Architecture School in Berlin from 1798; it was here that he came under the influence of the young architect Friedrich Gilly. In spite of this train-ing, he practised initially as a painter, and his work in this field is of the

first order. In 1803, the young Schinkel travelled to Italy, visiting Sicily and Rome, before finally travelling back to Berlin via Paris in 1805. This kind of 'Grand Tour', undertaken immediately after university graduation, and often lasting three or more years, was by no means unusual for young men of Schinkel's social class. His design work was at first limited largely to stage and set design, together with making dioramas (small-scale three dimensional models). This was a consequence of the stringency of the economic climate during the Napoleonic Wars; little money was available to construct new buildings. In 1810, he was appointed as the artistic adviser to the *Oberbaudeputation*, an organization which served a similar purpose to that of the Viennese *Hofbaurat*, in that

ABOVE: *Johann Erdmann Hummel (1769–1852):* Die Granitschale im Lustgarten in Berlin *(The 'Granite Shell' in the Pleasure Gardens in Berlin), oils on canvas, 1831. Berlin's Lustgarten served as a public pleasure park which reflected Biedermeier nostalgia for the rural life and all things natural.*

it authorized and supervised almost all building work of any significant scale in the region. Its powers, like those of its Austrian counterpart, were very far-reaching; in addition to approving plans for new buildings, it had to be consulted regarding alterations to and restorations of historic buildings. Schinkel worked his way up through the organization until 1838, when he was appointed director-in-chief, a position which gave him as an individual remarkable power over architecture in the state of Prussia. Unlike his Viennese opposite number, Peter von Nobile, however, it is clear that Schinkel's was a genuinely innovative and original talent.

Schinkel's work extends from painting, furniture design, interior design, through to architecture for the Prussian Monarchy and the administration. It is in this last sphere that he left his distinctive mark on the city of Berlin; both in his capacity as director of the *Oberbaudeputation*, and in his own work as an architect. His most productive period occurred in the years between 1815 and 1835, during which time he undertook many commissions for members of the Prussian Royal Family. He supplied designs for the Pavilion in the grounds of Schloß Charlottenburg for Friedrich Wilhelm III in 1824 to 1826, Prince Karl's palace in 1827, and Prince Albrecht's palace in 1830 to 1832. Schinkel also contributed to the moves by the *Oberbaudeputation* to improve quality and design in Prussian industry; moves which were very similar in nature to those undertaken in Vienna at the same time.

Schinkel's dealings with the Prussian Royalty were not always happy or productive, however; he had to wait four years, until 1839, for the go-ahead for a library from the King. Later in the same year, permission was withdrawn, illustrating the fickleness of the court politics under which Schinkel had to work. Drawings of various other projects – some of them surviving, some demolished, and some never built – were published by Schinkel from the years 1820 to 1840, accompanied by his own explanatory text. These were lavish engravings and lithographs, whose importance was such that they were re-published in a collected edition in 1858, 17 years after Schinkel's death.

Karl Friedrich Schinkel clearly used his considerable influence to the best effect; he was a versatile, ambitious and pioneering architect, who was able to take the best elements of the neo-Classical tradition in which he was educated, and attempt a bold synthesis with new aesthetic ideas, such as the Gothic Revival. The fusion of new and old that he envisaged both pre-empted, and was more profound than, the later Historicism which swept through architecture and interior design in Europe. Because of this quality, Schinkel appears to fit uneasily into any historical or stylistic pigeon-hole; he created his own, and at the same time transcended it. His feeling for the integration of structure with decoration, however, and his recognition of the importance of both, puts him in the same broad category of attitudes to applied art and design as the very best of the Austrian Empire craftsmen. Thus his work can be described as being at the heart of the Biedermeier philosophy.

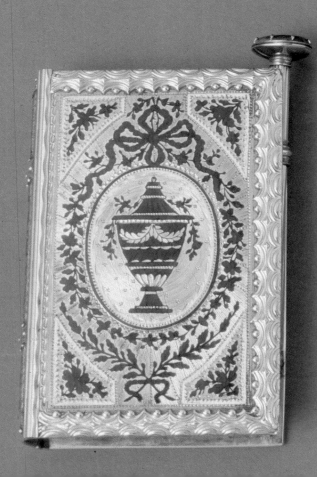

SIX

DECORATIVE AND APPLIED ARTS IN THE BIEDERMEIER ERA

The crafts in the Biedermeier era are most eloquently manifested in the glassware and ceramics, and of course the furniture, which have already been discussed in earlier chapters. There were however other types of decorative and applied arts which are worthy of attention. Many of the salient features and currents which had emerged and begun to influence both the organization of the industries and the actual objects produced were common to all of these forms of creativity. Textiles, together with fashion, metalwork, and printed illustration, all changed to some degree during the period, due to the increasing industrialization and the expansion of home and export markets.

THE TEXTILES INDUSTRY

The centre of the Austrian textiles industry in the first half of the eighteenth century was without doubt Schottenfeld, an area just outside Vienna. Its nickname among the Viennese was the *Brilliantengrund*, or Diamond Ground, because of the success of the silk trade there. Around the turn of the century, there were more than 30,000 people employed in textiles manufacture, primarily in silk weaving, and by 1822 around 600 companies were registered as being active there. The history of the industry's success can be traced back to the last two decades of the previous century, when individual weavers were encouraged by the authorities to settle there. Over the following 70 years, the textile trade changed almost beyond recognition, from a small-scale, highly-skilled, labour-intensive and fairly dispersed craft, to a highly-mechanized, semi-skilled, capital-intensive and geographically concentrated industry. This was a pattern which repeated itself across cabinet-making, and, to a rather lesser extent, glass manufacture, as we have seen in earlier chapters. The preponderance of outworkers, working from home at piece rates, which characterised much of the activity in textiles across Europe in the late eighteenth century, had created a highly competitive market, but not one in which a significant reduction in prices could be made without a loss of real income for the individual weavers. The arrival of machinery, however, brought about a new breed of entrepreneur, one who employed other workers to operate powered looms which enabled much greater productivity.

The Jacquard loom was one of the most important early inventions in the trade; it had been developed in Lyons in 1805, and was soon revolutionizing weaving across Europe. It arrived first in Vienna in 1816. The next major breakthrough came in the shape of a businessman named Christian Georg Hornbostel (1778–1841). It was he who managed to modify the most advanced mechanized looms used in the British cotton trade to weave silk, Vienna's traditional speciality. This was the first time this had been achieved, and it represented a major coup for Hornbostel and the Viennese silk trade generally. The mechanized looms required far less manpower, as little as one sixth of that of the conventional technology. Clearly, this spelt trouble for the established master weavers; the result was not an immediate wave of destitution in the industry, however, so much as an expansion of the market. Silks had become far cheaper, and their market had spread further down the social scale, than ever before, again mirroring the general trends in the woodworking and other trades. As a direct result of the introduction of the Jacquard loom, complex, figured silks became available to the middle class customer for the first time. Looms driven by steam power, which further amplified the economies of scale for the large mills, were first used in Austria in the mid-1820s.

Hornbostel's company continued to thrive until 1890, and he was involved in the *Allgemeine Österreichische Gewerbs-Produkten-Ausstellungen* (General Austrian Craft Products Exhibitions) of 1835, 1839, and 1845, which promoted the adoption of technology and machinery into industry in the region in order to help it compete with other nations' industries. In addition to this official, government-sponsored promotion of quality and modern factory methods in all branches of the crafts, there was also the Royal Imperial Woollen Textiles Factory, which had existed in Linz ever since 1672. It was brought under government ownership in 1754, and finally closed in 1850.

FASHIONS IN BIEDERMEIER AUSTRIA

The centre for the introduction and dissemination of the latest fashions in the Austrian Empire was naturally Vienna. The rapidity of changes in taste, and the impulsive and mercurial nature that the fashion trade has always exhibited existed in abundance in Biedermeier fashions, helped no doubt by the new wealth and self-confidence of the bourgeoisie. This helps us to date developments in this field quite precisely, for whereas changes in tastes in furniture tended, according to the nature of the subject, to be gradual and diffused, the new season almost inevitably brought about a new look in clothes. This is especially, although not exclusively, true of women's clothes; men's clothes, by contrast, tended to develop in a process which was at the same time slower and less systematic. The most striking innovation was the emerging independence of Vienna as a centre of fashion; until the mid-1820s at least, all the most respected dressmakers would make an annual sojourn to Paris to view the latest creations there. After this point, however, a distinctive Viennese style began to form separately from the French taste.

This development of a Viennese style was promoted by the *Wiener Modezeitung* (Viennese Fashion Journal), which was founded in 1816, by Johann Schickh, the proprietor of a fashion shop in the city. It was re-named the *Wiener Zeitschrift für Kunst, Literatur, Theater und Mode* (Viennese Journal of Art, Literature, Theatre and Fashion), a year later, and continued to inform the fashion-conscious Viennese citizen of the latest styles for another three decades, concentrating on the work of the city's own dressmakers and tailors. It featured superb, hand-coloured

ABOVE: A pattern card submitted to the National Factory Products Cabinet by a textiles factory near Vienna, dated 1824. Many of the vivid and colourful fabrics of the Biedermeier era can be seen in their original intensity and contrasts, protected from light and dust over the years in such pattern books, which were produced by the weavers and printers to advertise their products.

engravings of the contemporary fashions, made from drawings by the well-respected portrait artist Johann Nepomuk Ender (1793–1854) and the pre-eminent Viennese stage costume designer Philipp von Stuben-rauch (1784–1848), and executed by the engraver and etcher Franz Stöber (1795–1858). There is no doubt that the journal exerted consider-able influence over the trade, as well as providing a detailed record of even the slightest variations of clothes styles throughout the period. The duration of its existence coincides almost precisely with the generally agreed limits of the Biedermeier age; after a succession of editors, it ceased publication after the revolution, a victim of the renewed enthu-siasm with which press censorship was pursued after that time. In its heyday though, the journal had served as the litmus paper of all aspects of Viennese culture.

It comes as a slight surprise to an English-speaking reader to find that women's fashions in the Austrian Empire in the period leading up to and bordering on what we would term the Victorian era (1837–1901) were rather less prudish and conservative than their British counterparts. The obsessive concern with moral purity that insisted that men's breeches be referred to as 'unmentionables', and that bowdlerized ver-sions of classic literature be produced, abridged and cleaned up for family

consumption, had yet to afflict the German-speaking nations to any great degree. Consequently, plunging necklines, and hems above the ankle, were not uncommon, as well as garters embroidered with mildly suggestive wording; *Mein Wunsch – Ihr Glück* (My wish – Your Happiness), for instance. The characteristic item of women's clothing from the Biedermeier era must however be the shawl. This was developed along the lines of Indian cashmere shawls, in soft wool of contrasting hues, which were at first imported (at great expense), and later imitated, using a wool and silk mixture. Oriental motifs were also popular, as well as patterns copied from English and French textiles. The introduction of the Jacquard loom had enabled manufacturers to offer a much greater range of more complex patterns at an affordable price, and this was reflected in the vogue for the busy, intricate designs used in shawls. It contrasted with the more restrained pale colours and white which were prominent in dress fabrics until the mid to late 1820s. Such emphasis was placed on the design of fabrics for shawls, in fact, that one of the largest manufacturers of this type of garment offered a yearly prize for students at the *Wiener Polytechnische Institut* for the best pattern. The shawl became more widely popular in the following years, and was particularly associated with the Austrian Empire due to its lucrative export trade in this item with neighbouring nations.

Colours in women's fashions underwent an about-turn in the 1820s, becoming bolder and contrasting more vividly. Again, the new possibility

BELOW & RIGHT: Two womens' bonnets, Viennese, c1830. BELOW: Probably made for cooler weather, this bonnet is beautifully made with decorative rather than functional ribbons while the other one, RIGHT, was almost certainly a summer bonnet, being lighter and more decorative.

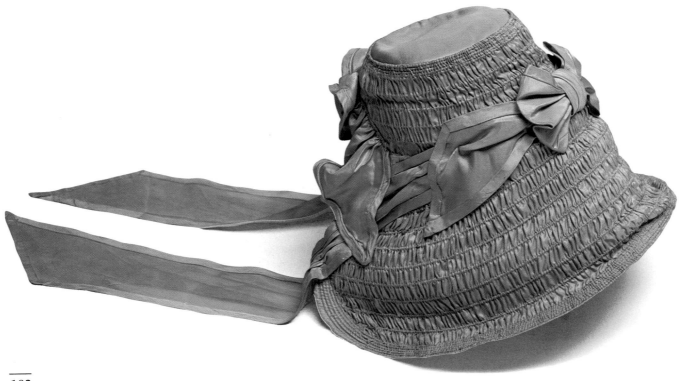

of weaving or printing more varied patterns in stronger colours, due in part to the technical advances of the time, was partly to blame for this change. The broad stripe design, often on a light ground with a contrasting flower or leaf motif down the centre, which had made its mark in furnishing fabrics, can be seen to have had its parallels in dress fabrics. From the beginning of the 1830s, quite large, open check designs, sometimes with a flower motif in the centre, and small flower patterns were popular, as were stylized oriental designs incorporating willow-pattern plate types of imagery. The new fondness for all things natural of course found its expression in fashion; in addition to the flower and leaf patterns already mentioned, embroidery and trimmings depicting flowers and foliage adorned dresses from the late 1820s onwards.

Fabrics for day wear were generally fine cottons, such as percale and poplin; for, evening dresses, organdie and the more expensive fabrics such as silks, in the form of tulle, were used. Lace, ribbon, braid and embroidered decoration became increasingly popular throughout the 1820s, but declined in the subsequent decade.

Shapes in women's clothes were equally subject to the occasionally abruptly changing tides of fashion. Waistlines, which had initially been very high, became lower and more pronounced during the second decade of the century, and as a result, the corset made a return, often in combination with a broad belt, emphasizing the silhouette. Meanwhile, skirts were becoming wider; the crinoline was introduced to Vienna by the leading dressmaker Josef Georg Beer (*b*1803) in 1838. Sleeves progressed from tailored styles at the start of the Biedermeier era, through to the heavily-padded versions typical of the mid-1830s. These in turn were eventually replaced by more moderate slit puff and flounce shapes.

By comparison with women's clothing, men's fashions were more stable and constant, although this is not to suggest in any way that clothes were unimportant. This was after all the era of the dandy, of Beau Brummell (1778–1840), and of elaborate dressing for display. Men's fashions in Vienna did not however follow the extravagant degree of narcissism which characterized Regency (1811–1820) fashions in Britain. Typical day wear consisted of a long frock coat in a dark hue, paler pantaloons (long trousers), a plain white shirt, and a contrasting waistcoat. Pantaloons, full-length tailored trousers which featured loops at the instep, had become acceptable formal wear for the first time in the

BELOW & RIGHT: An embroidered silk handbag and a beaded purse, Viennese, c1830.

period. For evening wear, however, the traditional knee-length breeches were still *de rigeur;* not until the mid-nineteenth century did black trousers become acceptable in this context. The waistcoat was the one item which permitted a large degree of self-expression; these often featured brightly-coloured or intensely detailed figured or shot silk designs.

METALWORKING

The Biedermeier era started at a low ebb for craftsmen working in precious metals. The trade had almost died out, and examples of work from previous generations had become scarce, due entirely to the effect of the Napoleonic Wars. During the wars all objects in precious metals were subject to an order from the government that they be handed over for melting down, to help pay for the war effort. This decree, surprisingly, seems to have been very widely complied with, and little work from the region around the turn of the century and before has survived. This left the gold- and silver-smithing trades in post-Congress Vienna in a very weak position, since most of the craftsmen had diversified or become destitute, and had not passed on their skills to a new generation of craftsmen. What little silverware and gold that was produced at the time was generally in the mould of the Empire Style; although as the industry began gradually to re-establish itself, a very pure, simple neo-Classicism emerged, replacing the intricate figurative ornament with austere, balanced form and proportion. Because of the expense of such pieces, however, they largely remained the preserve of the aristocracy, rather than the much larger bourgeoisie which dictated Biedermeier taste.

There was though a positive aspect to the decline of the precious metals trade, as it gave a much-needed boost to the other crafts which relied less heavily on valuable raw materials, such as the glass manufacturing and finishing described in an earlier chapter. Additionally, a patriotic custom arose of exchanging gold and silver for iron and bronze objects, thus reinforcing the region's traditional skills in crafting these materials.

Cast iron and bronze became particularly fashionable during the 1820s, and were used for an unlikely range of objects; jewellery, for instance, including earrings, bracelets, and necklaces, was very popular in the period. Bronze casting, in particular, virtually replaced the erstwhile position of gold; in its most refined forms, it was gilded and adorned with semi-precious mounts. Black-lacquered iron jewellery, and steel jewellery, had long been a Prussian speciality, and achieved extraordinary fineness and delicacy in the best examples, confounding prejudices of these materials as being heavy and cumbersome. Other cast iron and bronze objects included candlesticks, crucifixes, small picture frames, ink pots, and many more everyday items.

RIGHT: A Viennese silver urn. The precious metals trade had been decimated by a law which had been passed during the Napoleonic Wars, requiring all silver and gold articles to be handed in for melting down for the war effort.

ILLUSTRATIONS AND PRINTED MATTER

In the field of illustration in journals and books, the Biedermeier mentality is expressed quite clearly. The familiar preoccupations of home and family life, comfort, and nature were recurring themes in the pub-

lications of the time. Engravings, which in some cases were hand-coloured (such as in the Viennese Fashion Journal), and lithographs were popular.

Photography, although a technology in its infancy, was not unheard of at this time. Indeed, it was the discovery made by a Bavarian scientist, Heinrich Schulze (1687–1744) in Nuremberg in 1727, of the sensitivity of silver salts to exposure to light, that inspired a later generation of scientists to attempt to capture images reliably in this way. Towards the end of the period, primitive early photographic techniques, including Daguerrotypes and calotypes, were being experimented with throughout the German-speaking states. Carl-August von Steinheil (1801–1877) was one such experimenter; his images of Munich townscapes and occasional portraits from the years around 1840 onwards provide a fascinating, if somewhat murky, view of Bavarian life from one-and-a-half centuries ago.

Photography however had yet to emerge as a practical means of mass communication, and illustrations therefore continued to serve a central role in disseminating visual information of all types. Fashion illustrations, depictions of society life, views of landmarks in Vienna and other cities, craftsmen's pattern books, catalogues and trade cards, and views of interiors were all popular forms, as were views of Vienna's citizenry enjoying themselves in its two parks, the Prater and the Augarten. Illustrations served a similar function to literature, in that they commented on contemporary mores and fashions, often in a humorous or satirical manner. Needless to say, this attracted the attention of the official censor, in the form of the Royal Imperial Central Book Checking Office, to which all pictorial material for publication had to be sent for approval. The distinction between fine art – in the form of oil paintings – and popular published illustration became increasingly blurred, with the increased popularity of water colours, gouache paintings, and hand-coloured copperplate engravings. Additionally, engravers often worked from paintings by well-known artists, enabling a much wider section of the population to enjoy the visual arts.

Engravings were issued in folio editions, on large individual sheets usually incorporating a simple decorative border and a title or caption at the foot of the page; this was an especially common format for city views and prints commemorating particular events. A strong sense of civic pride emerges from the former; it is probable that they were intended, like the painted decorative glasses, for the tourist market as well as for the local inhabitants. Other themes crop up, such as idealized portraits of anonymous citizens such as 'The Washer Woman', or 'A Viennese Waiter'. Caricaturists such as Johann Christian Schöller (1782-1851) had a field day with the fads and fashions of the day; the craze for dancing was a particular target of their scorn. Because of the intrusion of the censor, satirists such as Schöller tended to concentrate on non-political subjects, or made at best oblique and generalized comments on the reality of poverty and destitution which continued to afflict certain sections of society. The nature of their observations would perhaps be best described as sarcastic, since the humour they contained was rather leaden.

Another source of illustrative material, and one which became very widespread through the Biedermeier era, was the sending of greetings cards, whether at New Year or in any other season. The Christmas card had not caught on at this time, and was, in fact, a British invention, from 1843.) Cards from this period are remarkable for their diversity, and their ingenuity in coming up with relatively cheap and simple novel features. The plainest usually featured short messages and were straight-forward black-on-white designs, albeit with fancy lettering and scrolls. Messages invariably bore either patriotic slogans (until the Congress of Vienna), or sentimental testimonials of friendship, love and loyalty; *Altar der Freundschaft* (Altar of Friendship), and *Fest wie ein Fels ist meine Treue* (Solid as a rock is my Faithfulness) are two typical examples. Far more common than the plain designs were cards with some form of colour, usually applied by hand over a printed outline. Embossed designs, where the design stands out in low relief against the background, were typical of the earlier part of the century, and often exhibit no printing at all. Their subject matter tended to reflect the influence of the Empire Style, incorporating urns, wreaths, cupids, and other neo-Classical motifs. The allusion to classical antiquity was further suggested by their appearance, which called to mind sculpted marble reliefs. Embossing was also combined with colour to give illustrative cards a three-dimensional appearance, and embroidered inset panels adorned the more elaborate designs. Visual puns and images composed of smaller images – Napoleon in profile, for instance, with the Prussian Eagle as his hat – recur in endless variations. The most spectacular cards featured pop-up or movable elements, which were contrived to alter the image or reveal some hidden detail.

SEVEN

BIEDERMEIER ART: PAINTING IN OILS AND WATERCOLOURS

It is significant that, not long after it had been coined as a description of bourgeois conservatism and insularity in a general social and political sense towards the end of the nineteenth century, the term Biedermeier was applied to the painting of that time. In the intervening period, however, the whole concept had been re-examined, and was regaining its former academic and cultural credibility. Several monographs on Biedermeier art appeared in the first two decades of the twentieth century, all of them written in German. Paradoxically, it is in the field of painting that a distinctive, self-contained phase of unmistakably Biedermeier creativity is in fact most difficult to pin down, despite the relative wealth of literature which has subsequently been produced on the subject. The artists of the era were working in a context which, although clearly influenced by the broader social and political currents of the time, had different imperatives and a different tradition to that of the contemporary cabinet-makers or other craftsmen. There were however certain artists, and certain developments, which have emerged as being characteristic of the period.

Fine art went through a process of change which was triggered by changes in the social structure of the Austrian Empire, and which parallelled developments in the crafts. The traditional patrons of the arts, the aristocracy and royalty, became less important, and a larger and more diverse market opened up for artists. The majority of the new patrons were successful merchants and bureaucrats; the wealthier bourgeoisie. Naturally, the themes, styles, and subject matter of paintings began to be adapted to their aspirations and preoccupations. For the first time, the middle classes could afford to indulge in collecting works of art, albeit on a modest scale. This affected even the media in which artists worked; watercolours and gouache paintings enjoyed a boom in popularity, which was attributable at least in part to the fact that they were

considerably less time-consuming and required less expensive materials than oils.

Surprisingly, even the technological innovations of the day left their mark on painting, unlikely though this may now seem. The camera obscura – a device which projected an image on to a screen, from where it could be traced – had been known and used by artists in the region for some time. When in the 1830s the basics of this device were combined with light-sensitive silver salts, the modern-day camera was born. Painting had since the seventeenth century generally been developing into a more and more realist and figurative discipline; but with the invention of photography, the need for such precise skills of observing and reproducing visual images by hand became less important. Painting therefore became less rigid and formal, and more concerned with conveying atmosphere and impressions; culminating, of course, in the French Impressionist painting of the 1870s. (The term 'Impressionist' had been coined as a derogatory description of one of Claude Monet's paintings by a critic in 1874; in this way, it neatly parallels the history of the term 'Biedermeier'.)

The main source of inspiration for many of the artists of the Biedermeier era was without doubt the painting of the Dutch masters of the seventeenth century. They had provided models of skill in draughtmanship and the use of light and shadow to communicate form. Indeed, many of Austria's artists, even the well-established ones, earned a sizable proportion of their income by producing direct copies of, or paintings after the style of, their Dutch predecessors.

Artistic endeavour was encouraged in Vienna by its cosmopolitan atmosphere and above all by its Academy of Fine Arts, which was the source of many of the period's greatest talents. Even in the capital of the Austrian Empire, however, artists needed to be versatile in order to make a reasonable living; it was rarely sufficient for a painter to rely on commissions and studio work alone. Several highly regarded painters were employed by the Royal Imperial Porcelain Factory, for instance, and undertook commissions for illustrations on ceramic plaques, plates, and dinner services, a less straightforward medium than oils on canvas. Other artists were commissioned by the journals of fashion and society life, to produce the original illustrations from which the engravers could work. Many of the greatest watercolour artists of the time had had humble beginnings, working as colourists on published engravings and

LEFT: Johann Wilhelm Preyer (1803–89): Still life, oils on canvas, signed and dated 1834. The direct influence of the Dutch masters of the 17th century is clear in this painting, both in its choice of subject and its treatment; note for instance the overall lighting, and the relish with which the detail of the flesh of the plum in the foreground has been painted.

RIGHT: Casper Johann Nepomuk Scheuren: The Artist with his Students on the Rhine, oils on canvas.

lithographs. Additionally, painters such as Balthasar Wigand (1770–1846) created minutely detailed gouache works, rather like larger miniatures, which depicted views of Vienna, or commemorated events such as the visit of Empress Caroline Augusta in 1816, and which were often specifically intended for embellishing craft objects, such as dressing table mirrors and writing cases. These examples all indicate the broader cultural and industrial changes which were afoot. The fine artist of the Austrian Empire was all too often caught awkwardly between seeking the high status of an expressive, individualistic academic painter, and the reality of having to work as a craftsman in order to make ends meet.

THEMES IN BIEDERMEIER PAINTING

Themes and subject matter in painting mirrored the preoccupations of contemporary literature and applied art to a large degree. Consequently, interior scenes, both with and without figures, feature heavily, indicating the importance that was attached to the home. Sentimental scenes from family life also figure prominently; these often followed variations on a well-worn theme of idealized domestic bliss, such as family gatherings, children playing, and morning prayers, which were all popular subjects, if not particularly challenging for either artist or viewer. It is from these detailed pictures, though, which usually illustrate scenes in typical middle class Biedermeier homes, that we gain such a clear image of taste and fashions in the clothes and interior decoration of the day.

Other genre paintings contained a narrative – the key to which is usually in the title – depicting some aspect of contemporary life; there was invariably an element of implied morality or criticism of contemporary mores. Soldiers departing for duty, and returning home, are the common subject of many paintings early in the Biedermeier era; not surprisingly, since during the Napoleonic Wars, this would have been a situation known to many families. Military themes, including individual soldiers as well as battle scenes, occur frequently in the painting of this early period. In stark contrast to these were the vivid flower paintings which were a speciality of a number of Viennese artists, including Josef Nigg (1782-1863), who in addition to painting in oils and watercolours, also supplemented his income by working for the Royal Imperial Porcelain Factory in Vienna. His work in porcelain, in the form of decorative

ABOVE: *Friedrich Wilhelm Moritz (1783–1855): Lake Geneva, pencil and watercolour.*

vases and plaques, mirrors his work on canvas and card, in that it features intense and highly accomplished paintings of flowers, often devoid of any background, or set against an otherwise very muted still life composition.

Another subject which crops up regularly in paintings of the period is that of anonymous, often rural, artisans and labourers, featuring in full-length portraits, set against a suitably naturalistic backdrop. This suggests the nostalgic and idealized view harboured by wealthy city-dwellers of country life.

Landscape paintings of the undeniably beautiful natural scenery which surrounded Vienna, and which was found in many other parts of the Austrian Empire, were perennial favourites; in this context, the work of Rudolf Alt (1812–1905), known as Rudolf von Alt, and Ferdinand Waldmüller deserves mention. Von Alt, who was the son of the painter Jakob Alt and the brother of the painter Franz Alt, was a versatile and talented artist. He used a variety of types of subject, from flower paintings and still lives, through to portraits, and also occasionally worked in oils, but is now remembered mostly for his spectacular landscape paintings. His career spanned a remarkable phase in the history of European art and design history; he began developing a distinctive style early in life, towards the end of the 1820s, and within a decade was one of the most highly respected painters of the time. He continued to innovate and develop right through the turmoil of the 1848 Revolution, the Crimean wars, and the quite different upheaval which followed the advent of Impressionism in the 1870s. He lived to witness the establishing of the Vienna Secession, and Austria's emergence into the modern age of design.

Like von Alt, Ferdinand Georg Waldmüller (1793–1865) specialized in expansive and dramatic views of Austrian landscape, although his favourite medium was oils rather than watercolours. His work in this area is characterized by his superb use of sharp tonal and colour contrasts against backgrounds of more muted hues and tones to give a feeling of immense depth to his pictures. Another of Waldmüller's favourite themes was the genre scene, in which an allegorical situation was depicted; he brought a particularly melodramatic style to bear on these paintings, with expressions and postures which were deliberately exaggerated for effect. As with so many of his contemporaries, Waldmüller was also active as a portrait artist too.

A contemporary of Waldmüller's, and an artist whose work is perhaps more illustrative of the Biedermeier attitude, was Josef Franz Danhauser (1805–1845). The son of the successful furniture factory owner Josef Danhauser, Danhauser junior studied at the Academy (and later taught there) from 1820 to 1826. He fluctuated in his career between painting and furniture design, taking over his father's business for a short time. His genre paintings include highly sentimental pictures of children and animals, and scenes from bourgeois life, which were more in keeping with the general concerns of that group, than for instance Waldmüller's rather grand and austere rendering of the Austrian landscape. The scenarios also feature figures in more naturalistic poses, and tend towards observation of scenes from everyday life, rather than allegorical reconstructions.

Peter Fendi (1796–1842) stood at the centre of a coterie of watercolour artists. His work often carried an implicit moral message, concentrating as it did on ordinary people in poverty and distress, or faced with difficult situations. It was this ability to tap a common nerve – the fear of financial ruin, for instance, or bereavement due to war – which endeared him to Biedermeier society; his portrayals of these scenes manage to avoid the overtly judgemental or sentimental attitude of some of his contemporaries, and used a language of symbolism from everyday life, which was clearly accessible to his audience. One of Fendi's friends and proteges, Carl Schindler (1821–1842), predicted in his short career the rise of a more dynamic and less formal style of painting, one whose aim was to communicate movement and time, rather than being restricted to a rigid, static representation. His watercolours of military life concentrate less on the traditional, grand-scale detailed depictions of battles and military victories, and more on individual soldiers in their normal lives. His selective use of colour and detail, to lead the eye into the centre of the action, and his fondness for allowing the tone of the paper to show through, helped establish a distinctive style and method in watercolour painting, one which freed it from the constraints of being an ersatz oil-on-canvas technique.

SCULPTURE

Sculpture was less able to adapt to the new social, political and economic conditions of the Biedermeier era than painting. The traditional patrons of the art, the monarchy, aristocracy and government, were unwilling to commission great works after the Congress of Vienna, for financial reasons more than any others. For sculptors, this problem of the official austerity of the period – also reflected in contemporary architecture – was compounded by a general disinclination toward displays of ostentation which had set in after the demise of the Empire Style. Of all of the arts, sculpture is the most public; and the new concentration on the private, domestic sphere no longer favoured such grand gestures to the outside world. Having said this, the defeat of Napoleon clearly called for a certain number of commemorative statues and monuments in the years immediately following the Congress. This work generally exhibited strong influences of the heavy, formal neo-Classicism of the Empire Style; winged spirits, cornucopiae and cupids are common features, as well as references to Greek mythology.

As in other fields where the language of Classicism had been applied rather too literally, there are occasionally outlandish anachronisms. Joseph Dialer's (1797–1846) Spirit of 1809, for instance (1809 being the year in which Napoleon had been defeated at Aspern) depicts Clio, the winged muse of history, with his tablet and shield, together with a contemporary musket casually propped by his side. The technical skill of the creator was particularly important, as it had been in Rococo, and was demonstrated in details such as lavish folds of fabric. Sculpture was given a boost by occasional large commissions – Archduke Charles for instance commissioned works from Joseph Klieber (1773–1850), the director of the Viennese School of Engraving, for Schloß Weilburg, and his city residence, Albertina, which again show Rococo tendencies. The architect Karl Friedrich Schinkel also commissioned sculptures to embellish his buildings for the Prussian government and Royal Family in Berlin; after delays and a certain amount of procrastination on the part of the King, these too were executed and installed.

EIGHT

CONCLUSION: THE BIEDERMEIER LEGACY

Some time ago, an anthology of the decorative arts published in Britain dedicated just one paragraph to its entry on the Biedermeier style, describing it as being vulgar and tasteless, a fashion of the philistine *nouveaux riches* of central Europe in the early nineteenth century. This attitude, although unusually harsh in its choice of words, was for a long time typical of the English-speaking world's conception of the style. Indeed, up until the last decade, it had been virtually ignored. There was a feeling that the styles were insubstantial and derivative, somehow creating a visual reflection of the political nature of the era. The focus of interest remained the orthodox styles and their proponents – Empire, Sheraton, and Baroque. Biedermeier, heralding as it did the arrival of the modern period in furniture, textiles and other craft production, presented too easy a target for critics. It lent itself to being characterized – or caricatured – as the end of the era of great craftsmanship and the slide into mass production. Historians of furniture tend to resent particularly the populist aspects of Biedermeier, and often see it as a diluted and cheapened Empire style, lacking the individual conviction and vision of 'genuine' neo-Classicism.

Biedermeier has enjoyed consistent popularity on its home ground.

LEFT:
A bed in the Biedermeier style, Danish, c1920. The crafts of the Biedermeier era influenced a wide range of furniture designers, both directly and indirectly, in the early years of this century.

After its fall from grace in the period immediately following the revolution of 1848, it made a come-back as a formative influence on the work of architects and designers such as those in the Vienna Secession in 1897. This was a collection of like-minded artists and craftsmen, led by Gustav Klimt (1862–1918), and including among its associates Josef Hoffmann (1870– 1956).

The binding philosophy of the Secessionists was the unification of the arts and crafts; it was a theme which the Biedermeier architect Karl Friedrich Schinkel both preached and practised in his work. The work of the Secessionists was very much in the Art Nouveau style popular at the time. The return to simplicity and the use of forms inspired by the natural world demonstrate the influence of Biedermeier furniture on Art Nouveau. In searching for an aesthetic for the new century, craftsmen of the time even copied Biedermeier pieces. The striking penchant for theatricality of effect with practicality of production, which Art Nouveau inherited from Biedermeier, is most clearly evidenced in the decorative ironwork designed by Hector Guimard for the Paris Métro. These structures, which appear to exhibit little symmetry, are in fact identical cast-iron sections bolted together.

The Vienna Secession was succeeded by the *Wiener Werkstätte* (the Viennese Workshops), which were set up as a co-operative commercial enterprise in 1903, under Josef Hoffmann and several of his Secessionist colleagues. Certain of its products, in particular the metalwork, retained the distinctive stamp of Biedermeier.

Biedermeier continued to exert an influence, either directly, or mediated through other styles which had themselves been influenced by it, after the First World War and into the 1920s. Both vernacular and avant-garde architects and designers looked to the work of Biedermeier designers such as Josef Danhauser and Michael Thonet for inspiration. The Art Deco style saw the arrival of a heavier design and more solid aesthetic than that of Art Nouveau, and one which was more widely taken up by manufacturers and the public alike. It exhibits many of the elements of Biedermeier, especially in its furniture designs, which emphasize simple curves and bold, simple forms. The Art Deco preference for regular geometric solids can be seen as a development of the direction in which Biedermeier had been moving before the onset of the Rococo revival. It is this similarity that gives some Biedermeier furniture designs their remarkably modern appearance.

A modern interpretation of the Biedermeier style: a coffee table in birchwood and masur birch, designed by Rupert Cavendish and Benedict Critchley.

Biedermeier also provided a source for key figures in avant-garde design in the inter-war period. Michael Thonet's bentwood and laminated furniture in particular was a model of both design simplicity and production efficiency which the architects and designers of the Modern Movement were striving to achieve. The Swiss architect Le Corbusier, (1887–1965), was especially fond of the simple bentwood side chair from the Thonet range, and used it frequently in his designs. It was the simplicity and purity of this design that partly inspired the early experiments in tubular steel chairs undertaken by Mart Stam and Marcel Breuer during the 1920s. The latter's work at the Bauhaus was in fact taken up by the Thonet company and put into production; copies of his original cantilever chair are still widely available today.

The Biedermeier era was a quite unique period in the history of decorative and applied arts in Europe. It followed a decade and a half of ruinous war, and took place against a backdrop of a politically repressive and thoroughly anti-progressive government, who were prepared to go to almost any lengths to perpetuate their reign and the influence of their ideas. At the same time, the upheavals associated with the Industrial Revolution over the period of more than a century were reflected in profound social and cultural change. All this hardly sounds like the ideal environment in which to germinate a new style of design and a new attitude to the crafts, and yet, paradoxically, it produced a wealth of superb objects. It may be that the state of flux in the region at the time, combined with the particular preoccupations of the populace, created a kind of dynamic instability which favoured expression predominantly in the crafts rather than in music, literature, or politics.

In conclusion, the brief overview of the art and design of the Biedermeier age that this book seeks to give should make it clear that Biedermeier was a distinctive and highly influential visual style, but was also more than just this; it was the expression of an attitude to life in a period of fundamental change. The clarity and precision of the architecture of Karl Friedrich Schinkel, the inventiveness and imagination of the furniture designs of Josef Danhauser, and the workmanship and skill of the glassware of Anton Kothgasser all stand as superlative manifestations of creativity in their own right. They also however give us an insight into the psychology of a society which was in many ways the prototype for modern Western nations, and which was to alter the course of history in the following decades.

I N D E X

A

Academy of Fine Arts, Vienna, 24, 38, 49, 72, 76, 81, 82, 84, 113
Akademie der Bildenen Künste, 24
Albertina, palace of, 81, 120
Allgemeine Österreichische Gewerbs-Produkten-Ausstellungen, 39, 74, 99
Alt, Rudolf von, 118
Annagelb/Annagrün, 66
architecture, 55, 79-85, 94
Art Deco, 124
Art Nouveau, 58, 124
ash furniture, 44
Austrian Empire, 10, 16, 18, 29, 31
Austrian Museum of Art and Industry, 58

B

Bad Ischl (Thomas Ender), **121**
Bärentzen, Emilius, **90**
Baroque influence on furniture and interior desing, 13, 29, 51, 55
Bavaria, glassware trade in, 61, 62
beakers, glass, **11, 60,** 66-7, **70, 71,** 74
beds and bedrooms, 47, 89-90, **122**
beech furniture, 34, 44, 51
Beer, Josef Georg, **100,** 103
Beethoven, Ludwig van, 24
bentwood, 34, 44, 51, 53
Berlin, 53, 55, 57, **94,** 95
'Beidermaier, Herr Gottlob', 9, 18, 20
Beidermeier style
  decline and revival, 29, 58
  influence of, 13, 53, 58, 123-4
Biemann, Dominik, 68-9
birchwood furniture, **14, 16, 21, 27, 28, 39,** 44, **78, 84, 87,** 124
Bohemia, glassware trade in, 61-2, 63-4, 65, 67, 68
Bohemian Industrial Products Exhibition, 65

Böhm, August, 69
book illustration, 106, 108-9
Bouquoy, Graf von Longueval, 64, 65
bourgeoisie, growth of, 10, 13, 20, 26, 27, 29, 36, 112
bowls, glass, 67
brass, 46
Breuer, Marcel, 53
Brilliantengrund, 97
bronze, 46, 51, 106
building control, 82, 84, 94

C

cabinets, **30,** 44
calotypes, 108
camera obscura, 113
canary glass, 66
caricaturists, 109
carpets, **88,** 90
cast iron, 34, **54,** 55, 106
ceilings, **88,** 89
censorship, 10, 15, 18, 20, 25, 27, 29, 108, 109
ceramics, 61, **72, 73,** 74-7
chairs, **14, 21,** 44, **45,** 47, **51, 52, 54,** 89-90
Charles, Archduke, 81, 120
cherrywood furniture, 44
Cologne (Samuel Prout), **12**
clothing, 99-105
coloured glass, 65, 66
colours
  dress fabric, 102-3
  in interior design, 88-9
commodes, **17, 49, 84, 85**
composers, 24
Congress of Vienna, 10, 17, 58
copper and coloured glass production, 65
Court Architectural Committee (*Hofbaurat*), 82, 84
Couvertrahmen, 49, 90
cultural life, 18, 20, 24-5
curtains, 47, 49, **88,** 89-90

D

Daguerrotypes, 108
Danhauser, Josef, 26, 34, 47, 49-51

Danhauser, Josef Franz, 51, 119
Danhauser Furniture Factory, 7, 8, 86, 88
desks, **80, 85,** 86
Dialer, Joseph, 120
Diamond Ground, 97
drapery, 47, 49, **88,** 89-90
Dresden (William Wyld), **8**
dresses, **100,** 102-3
dressing tables, 89-90
dual-purpose furniture, 36, 50, **85**

E

ebony, substitutes for, 44
Egermann, Friedrich, **64,** 65
Eichrodt, Ludwig, 8
elm furniture, **14**
Empire style
  in furniture design, **21,** 31, 32, 34, 40, **40,** 46, 47
  in gold and silverware, 106
  in greetings card design, 109
  in sculpture, 120
enamel painting, 61, 69, 72, 74, **96**
Ender, Johann Nepomuk, 101
Ender, Thomas, **121**
English influences
  on furniture design, 40, 57
  on glassware production, 62, 63, 65, 67
engravings, 66, 68-9, 108-9
Etablissement für alle Gegenstände des Ameublements, 49

F

fabrics, 97-9
  dress, 102-3
  upholstery, **45,** 46-7, **88**
factory production, 24, 25, 34, 40, 49-50
family life, 10, 20
  influence on furniture design, 36
  as subject matter for illustration, 106, 108, 116
fashions, 99-105
Fendi, Peter, 119

Ferdinand I, Emperor, 29
Fliegende Blätter, 9
floorcoverings, **88,** 90
forming, wood, 51
France: influence on furniture design, 39-40, 49
  see also Empire style; Rococo
Francis I, Emperor, 17
Franz Josef I, 29, 80
Friedrich Wilhelm III, 55, 95
fruitwood furniture, **17, 44, 45**
functionalism
  in furniture design, 36, **37,** 47, 50, 55, 86
  in architecture, 82
furnishings, soft, 46-7, 49, **88,** 89-90
furniture, 7, 8, **14, 16, 17, 21, 26-8, 30,** 31-59, **78, 80, 83, 84,** 85-90, **122**

G

gardens and parks, 24, 91-2, **94,** 108
Caro, Johann, **76**
General Austrian Craft Products Exhibitions, 39, 74, 99
genre painting, 116, 119
Gentz, Friedrich von, 20
Germanic Confederation, 18, 29, 31
Gesswald, Friedrich, **76**
gilding, **11, 21, 30,** 46, **48,** 51, **59,** 61, 66, **75, 76**
Gilly, David, 55
Gilly, Friedrich, 55, 92
glass, **11,** 60-74, 76
glazing, glass, 66
Globustisch, 40, **41**
goblets, glass, 67
Goethe, Johann Wolfgang, 68, 91
gold, **96,** 106
Gothic influence on Biedermeier style, 29, 34, 55, **83,** 95
gouache painting, **23,** 61, **76, 77, 88, 93,** 108, 112-3, 116
Granitschale im Lustgarten in

Berlin (Johann Hummell), **94**
greeting cards, 109
Grillparzer, Franz, 25
Guimard, Hector, 124

H

Harrach factory, 62, 63-4, 65, 66
Heidelberg, view of (James Baker Payne), **9**
Herder, Johann Gottfried, 91
Historicism
  influence on architecture, 82, 95
  influence on furniture design, 29, 31, 34, 51, 53, 55, 57-8, **83**
Hofbaurat, 82, 84
Hoffmann, Josef, 13, 58, 124
Holl, Benedikt, 40
Hornbostel, Christian Georg, 98, 99
Hummel, Johann Erdmann, **94**
Huysum, Jan van, 76
Hyalith glass, 65

I

illustrations, book and journal, 106, 108-9
industrialization, 24, 25-6, 27, 29, 34, 40, 58, 98
interior design, 85-91
irish influence on glassware production, 92
iron
  cast, 34, **54**, 55, 106
  and coloured glass production, 65

J

Jacquard loom, 29, 98
jardinières, 25, **48**, 91
Jensen, Johann Laurents, **118**
jewellery, 106
Jugendstil movement, 58

K

Karoly Palace, 50
Klieber, Joseph, 120
Klimt, Gustav, 124
Kohberger, Johann, 110
König Ottokars Glück und Ende (Franz Grillparzer) 25
Kornhäusel, Josef, 81, 82
Kothgasser, Anton, **11**, 68, **70**, 72, 74
Krüppel, Heinrich, **88**
Kussmaul, Adolph, 8

L

laminating, wood, 26, 34, 51
landscape painting, **22**, 25, 118-9
Le Corbusier, 13, 53
Leistler, Carl, 51
Liechtenstein, Prince, 81
Liechtenstein Palace, 51, 53
literature, 25, 91
  see also censorship
lithographs, 108
Lobmeyr, Josef, 64, 67
Looms, Jacquard, 29, 98
Louis Seize style, 31, 32
Lythalin glass, 64, **64**, 65

M

mahogany furniture, **14, 30, 36-7, 38, 40**, 44, **48, 52, 83, 87**
maple, 44, **46**
marbling in glassware, 65
March Revolution, 27, 29
mechanization, 25-6, 29, 40, 98-9
metals and metalworking, 34, 46, 51, **54**, 55, 65, 66, **97**, 105-6, **107**
Metternich, Prince Clemens Lothar, 15-18, 20, 26, 29, 51, 82
middle class, growth of, 10, 13, 20, 26, 27, 29, 36, 112
Milchglas, 62
mirrors, **59**
Mohn, Gottlob Samuel, **60**, 68, 69, 72, 74
Moritz, Friedrich Wilhelm, **117**
mother of pearl, **59**
murals, 89
music, 24

N

Nachsommer, Der (Adalbert Stifter), **94**
National-Fabrikprodukten-kabinett, 38-9, 65, 69
nature, love of, **22**, 34-5, 91-3, 103
neo-Classicism, 31-2
  in architecture, 81, 82, 84
  in furniture design, **36**, 40, 42, **48**, 50, **54**
  in gold and silverware, 106
  in greetings card design, 109
  in interior design, 89
  in sculpture, 120
Niedermayer, Matthias, 76
Nigg, Josef, 76, 116-7
Nobile, Peter von, 82, 84, 94
Nuremberg (Samuel Prout), **6**

O

oak furniture, 44
Oberbaudeputation, 93-4, 95
oil painting, **19, 22, 90, 94**, 108, **110, 112**, 113, **114-5**, 118-9, **121**
opaque glass, **64**, 65
oriental designs, 102, 103

P

painting, 110-21
  on glass, 68, 69, **70-1**, 72, 74
  see also enamel; gouache; landscape; oil; watercolour
parks and gardens, 24, 91-2, **94**, 108
patent secretaires, **56**, 57, **57**, 86
patinated bronze, 46
patronage, 13, 24, 112, 120
pattern books, 26, 40, 63, **99**, 108
patterns
  dress fabric, 102, 103
  in interior design, 89
Payne, James Baker, **9**
pearwood, **35**, 44, **45**
Pelikan, Franz Anton, 69
pen and ink work, 44
photography, 108, 113
plant stands, 24, **48**, 91
poetry, 25, 91
Pohl, Franz, 65
Pohl, Johann, 64, 65
Pokal, 66
political climate, 10, 15-20
porcelain, 72, 73, 74-7
Prague Industrial Exhibitions, 68, 69
Pre-March era, **9**, 15-27
pressed glass, 67
Preyer, Johann Wilhelm, **112**
Prout, Samuel, **6, 12**
Prussia, 16, 18

R

Ranftbecher, **11, 60**, 66, **70, 71**, 74
Reichstadt, Duke of, **11**
religious buildings, 82
Renaissance style, 29, 51, 55
residential architecture, 79-81, 84-5
Riedel, Josef, 66
Rococo influence, 13, 29
  on furniture design, **30**, 32, **32**, 34, 39, 47, 51, 53, 58
  on glassware design, 62, 63
  on sculpture, 120
Romantic Movement, 24-5, 91
rosewood inlays, **27**, 84, 87

Royal Imperial Central Book Checking Office, 18, 108
Royal Imperial Porcelain Factory, Vienna, 76, 113, 116
Royal Imperial Woollen Textiles Factory, 99
Ruysch, Rachel, 76

S

satinwood inlays, **27, 84, 87**
Schadlbauer, Leopold, 74
Scheuren, Casper Johann Nepomuk, **114-5**
Schickh, Johann, 99
Schindler, Carl, 119-20
Schindler, Emil Jacob, **23**
Schinkel, Karl Friedrich, 8, 34, 53-5, 57-8, 92-5, 120, 124
Schloß Charlottenburg, 95
Schloß Laxenburg, 72
Schloß Weilberg, 26, 50, 81, 120
Schmidt, Carl, **59**
Schmidt, Karl, 24, 38
Schöller, Johann Christian, 109
Schottenfeld, 97
Schubert, Franz, 24
Scott, Sir Walter, 91
Screen Writing Table, 57
sculpture, 120
Secessionists, 124
'Second Rococo', 29, 34, 53, 58
secretaires. **14, 33, 34, 35**, 36, **36-7, 38, 40**, 44, **48**, 85
  fallfront, **26, 83**
  patent, **56**, 57, **57**, 86
settees, **14, 27, 32, 39**, 46-7, **47, 78**, 90
shawls, **101**, 102
Sheraton, Thomas, 40, 57, 86
silk, 97, 98, 102, 103
silver, 106, **107**
sofa tables, **21**
sofas, **14, 27, 32, 39**, 46-7, **47, 78**, 90
soft furnishings, 46-7, 49, **88**, 89-90
Sonntagsjager, Der (Carl Spitzweg), **19**
Sorgenthal, Conrad Sögel von, 76
spherical table, 40, **41**
Spirit of 1809 (Joseph Dialer), 120
spitoons, **46**
Spitzweg, Carl, **19**
Sprenger, Paul, 84
St Stephan's cathedral, Vienna, **11**, 64, 74
staining
  glass, 66

wood, 44
steel jewellery, 106
Steigerwald, Franz, 67, 68-9
Steinheil, Carl-August von, 108
Stifter, Adalbert, 25, 91
Stöber, Franz, 101
stools, **14, 44**
Strauß, Johann (the elder), 24
Stubenrauch, Philipp von, 101
Sturm und Drang writers, 25, 91
Sunday Hunter, The (Carl Spitzweg), **19**
Sunlight through Pine Trees (Emil Jacob Schindler), **23**

T

tables, **14, 16, 21**, 36, 40, **41, 47, 87**
tallboys, 28
Talleyrand, Prince Charles Maurice de, 17
Temple of Theseus (Peter von Nobile), 82
textiles, 29, 97-9, 102-3
Thonet, Michael, 26, 34, 51-3

tilt top tables, **87**

U

Überfanggläser, 66
upholstery, **45,** 46-7, 49, **88**
uranium and glass colour, 66
urbanization, 10, 25, 36
urns, **64, 107**

V

vases, glass, **11, 60,** 66, **70-1,** 74
veneers, 26, **26,** 34, **40,** 44, 46, 51, **52**
Vienna
Academy of Fine Arts, 38, 24, 49, 72, 76, 81, 82, 84, 113
building control, 80, 82
Congress of, 10, 17, 58
cultural life in, 18, 20, 24-5
as fashion centre, 99
furniture makers in, 36, 38-51
parks and gardens, 91-2, **93**

Polytechnical Institute, 24, 38, 82, 102
riots in, 29
Royal Imperial Porcelain Factory, 72, 76, 116
Vienna and the Viennese, in Pictures from Life (Adalbert Stifter), 25
Vienna Secession, 124
Viennese Customs Office and Provincial Revenue Administration Building, 84
Viennese Fashion Journal *see* Viennese Journal of Art...
Viennese Journal of Art, Literature, Theatre and Fashion, 99-101
Viennese Workshops, 124
View of Heidelberg (James Baker Payne), **9**
Voight, Adolph Friedrich, **56**
Vormärz era, 9, 15-27

W

Waldmüller, Ferdinand Georg, 118-9
wall coverings, 47, **88,** 89

walnut furniture, **17,** 44, **49,** 51, **52**
watercolour painting, **8, 23,** 88, 108, 112-3, 116, **117,** 118, 119-20
weaving, 29, 98-9
Wien und die Wiener, in Bildern aus dem Leben (Adalbert Stifter), 25
Wiener Moden Zeitung see Wiener Zeitschrift fur Kunst...
Wiener Polytechnische Institut, 24, 38, 82, 102
Wiener Werkstätte, 124
Wiener Zeitschrift fur Kunst, Literatur, Theater und Mode, 99-101
Wigand, Balthasar, **59,** 116
wood, 44
see also individual species
writing (authorship), 18, 20, 25, 91
Wundsam, Josef, **77**
Wyld, William, **8**

Y

yew furniture, 44